Endorsements for No Fishing in the Parking Lot

I have known Denver and Debbie Copeland since the late1980s. They are an example of how God can use people who honestly seek God's direction for their lives.

"No Fishing in the Parking Lot" is a book about God and how He used a pastor and his wife, a church and people that responded to God's call. It is an example of a couple that realized no matter where you live, you are on a mission field. God has people to be reached with the Gospel. It starts by getting out of our houses, churches and "parking lots". People do not know how much you care until you meet them where they are. As a pastor friend once said, "You go sit on their couches and they will come and sit on your pews".

Be careful reading this book. God may be calling you to stop fishing in the parking lot. The suggestions in this book may be what you need to penetrate the lostness in your area.

David N. Baldwin

Alaska Baptist Convention

Executive Director/Treasurer

T0156435

Denver first began telling us about Lighthouse Community Church in 2006 while we were serving together in Louisiana with SBC Disaster Relief. We were excited to learn he was already outlining this book. *No Fishing in the Parking Lot* is the account of a church and her pastor who, with faith and humility, submitted themselves to God's plan, became sensitive to His leading, and found wonderful, relevant and practical ways to show His love in their community. We're so glad to see their story in print at last and pray those who read it will be encouraged to "step out in faith" as they did - and meet needs in Jesus' name.

Larry and Marcia Hoffman

Illinois

"No Fishing in the Parking Lot" proves that when you rely on the Lord and His leadership great things can be accomplished. This book also proves that any congregation, any size can climb any size mountain when the leadership and membership are willing to step out in faith to follow God's direction. In my twenty plus years in the ministry and eleven years as a National missionary I have never met anyone like Denver and Deb Copeland or a church like Lighthouse Community church. As you read this book you will be amazed as I have been at what a small congregation in Nikiski, Alaska has accomplished because they were willing to follow God's direction no matter where it took them or what they had to do. See how coloring outside the lines with God's direction can lead to many lives being changed.

I would like to thank Denver, Deb and Lighthouse Community church for allowing World Changers to be a small part of what they did in Alaska. We look forward to what God is going to do in Hawaii as we continue the partnership. Thanks for the thousands of lives you have touched because you were willing to color outside the lines.

Jon Hodge

National Missionary

NAMB/World Changers

If you would like to see how a small church in a rural community grew to be one of the largest, less than 3 acres of land multiplied to 19 acres with a 6,000 square foot building increased to 26,000 square feet of buildings, on a budget of less than $80,000.00 that grew to over $165,000.00, from a hand full of ministries to over 50, for the last several years averaged 25 salvations & baptisms a year, and grew from 35-40 to approximately150-165 in attendance in a 12 year period in a declining population and economic base---you may want to read *"No Fishing in the Parking Lot"*. It is my prayer and desire that this would benefit just one pastor or church.

No Fishing In The Parking Lot

BY
Denver E. Copeland

Edited by
Deborah L. Copeland

Trafford Publishing
Bloomington, Indiana

Note for Librarians: A cataloguing record for this book is available from Library
and Archives Canada at www.collectionscanada.ca/amicus/index-e.html

Printed in Victoria, BC, Canada.

ISBN: 978-1-4269-1978-7 (sc)

ISBN: 978-1-4269-1979-4 (dj)

Library of Congress Control Number: 2009938321

*Our mission is to efficiently provide the world's finest, most comprehensive book publishing
service, enabling every author to experience success. To find out how to publish your book, your
way, and have it available worldwide, visit us online at www.trafford.com*

Trafford rev. 10/20/2009

 www.trafford.com

North America & international
toll-free: 1 888 232 4444 (USA & Canada)
phone: 250 383 6864 ♦ fax: 812 355 4082

Lovingly dedicated to our children
Norman Copeland
Kelli Copeland
Michelle Hall
Jeanette Tapley
Kimberly Curren

who through the years shared us with so many others

Also for those at Lighthouse Community Church
who were there from our beginning to end
and shared the work and vision with us.
JR & Vicki Hensley
Retha Hall-Veal
Hilda Spires
Jim & Marita Wolverton

Contents

Thank You
Service

PREFACE

I REALLY DON'T WANT TO TELL YOU ABOUT MY LIFE, but I do want to tell you what the Lord has done in Nikiski, Alaska. I feel it is important for you to know my background to understand how the Lord brought me to this ministry. The church He called me to is a church that in the early years of my ministry I would not have been interested in accepting a call to. I may have even been downright disobedient and not accepted the call. As I went through tough times and brokenness I realized it is a privilege that God would send me to this church and in this area for this work. Putting this account on paper is in obedience to Him as He has asked me to share what has happened at this church, with this group of people, with those who have willingly come to share with resources and talents. To God be all the glory!

In December of 1996, I became the Pastor of North Kenai Baptist Church, now known as Lighthouse Community Church. There were about thirty-five or forty people attending when we accepted the call.

Situated along a twenty-mile section of road, Nikiski is a small rural community of about five thousand people. It is south of Anchorage, Alaska on the Kenai Peninsula. The area has a very small economic base and has been declining in population for several years. In 1996, there were only eight protestant churches in the area. There were two elementary schools with about four hundred students each. Today there are ten churches, one elementary school with four hundred students, and a Junior/Senior High with approximately five hundred students. One company in this community that once employed approximately three hundred now employs less than a dozen. Hopes and prayers are that the economy turns around soon.

I have attempted to relate this story in a chronological order, but as events have intertwined over the years, it is impossible to separate them completely. Looking back, we can see how God moved among us and directed our interwoven paths, we hope you can too.

D.E.C. / August 2009

CHAPTER 1

God Brought Me Here

I WAS BORN NEAR DE SOTO, MISSOURI ON NOVEMBER 23, 1954. I was raised in an area outside of De Soto called Luckey. I attended the Luckey Baptist Church, which later became the First Baptist Church of Luckey.

When I was seven years old, I received Jesus Christ as my personal Lord and Savior. At the age of fifteen, I surrendered my life to the ministry. In March of 1970, I preached my first sermon at Luckey Baptist Church. Before the age of seventeen I was preaching youth revivals and singing in a quartet, which included my good friend, Rick Ferguson. We were friends all through elementary and high school. Later, Rick became the pastor of Riverside Baptist Church in Denver, Colorado. Rick and I shared many ministry ideas before he went home to be with the Lord on July 25, 2002.

After graduating from high school, I started attending Jefferson College in Hillsboro, Missouri. I had a full scholarship, but at that time I was unaware of any financial aid available to assist in the daily living costs associated with attending college. My parents were very poor and were unable to help me with any college expenses. Barely making ends meet, I found myself working at a truck stop. Working there forty- eight hours a week, going to school fulltime, and being a youth minister at Tabernacle Baptist Church in St. Louis, I was burning the candle at both ends. I decided to join the Air Force. My plan was to join for a term of four to six years and then I would be able to apply for the GI Bill to finish my school.

While in the military, I began to serve as Associate Pastor for churches in locations where I was stationed. After a time, I found myself serving as pastor at some of those places. Each time it was time to reenlist, I would pray about it and the Lord made it very clear to me that I should stay in. I was able to serve in the ministry while the military was paying the bills. I didn't have the financial burdens that some have in smaller churches

The Lord blessed and I was able to serve in churches in Germany, Colorado, Nevada, and Alaska. It was a great time for me. In 1983 I was stationed at Eielson Air Force Base in North Pole, Alaska. North Pole is about twelve miles from Fairbanks, Alaska. In 1986, I separated from the Air Force and joined the active duty Air National Guard. Finally, in February of 1994, I retired.

While at North Pole, I served in three churches. I was an Associate Pastor at Moose Creek Baptist Church, Pastor of the First Baptist Church in Fairbanks, and Associate Pastor at First Baptist Church North Pole. Those were tough times and some of the things that happened really shaped my life permanently. In fact, during my time in the area, I left the ministry for about three and a half years. More on this later. It was then my wife Debbie and I opened a business. Working six days a week and fourteen to sixteen hours a day, we attempted to make it a success.

A friend of mine, David Baldwin, the Director of Missions of the Tanana Valley Baptist Association, came into the store one day. As we were talking, he asked me if I would consider supply preaching for churches that were without pastors. I told him repeatedly that I couldn't and he knew the reason why. God kept after me for a whole year pursuing me to be obedient. I kept giving God all kinds of excuses for an entire year.

On a snowy night in March of 1995, Debbie and I attended a revival. We went to the altar to pray and it was there I surrendered it all to Him. I cried out to God. As I prayed, for the first time in my life I experienced brokenness. I have attempted to explain it to people, but words fail. It felt as if I was extremely dirty and then I walked into a good hot shower. As the water of the shower began to hit the top of my head, it cleansed perfectly all the way to the bottom of my feet. I felt the power of the Holy Spirit fill me from the bottom of my feet to the top of my head. I was tired of working for His approval; I was tired of running; and I would do whatever He wanted me to do. I began to see how God had been working on me for about a year to get back into the ministry. But I needed God to open the doors. I didn't want to open the doors myself. I told Him if He would open them, I would obey, gladly.

The very next day a friend of mine, Johnny McCoy, called me. He is the Pastor of First Baptist Church North Pole, Alaska, and has been serving there for thirty-five plus years in one capacity or another. A situation had occurred with a staff member and he said he needed immediate help. I knew I couldn't say "no" because I had told God, just the night before, if He opened the door I would walk through it. I told Johnny I could work four hours in the morning, and then I had to work my business the rest of the day.

The church called me as a Minister of Education to start with, and as God began to move, they called me as Associate Pastor. I could hardly believe it. I had been thinking that God would never use me, that the most I might ever be was a Sunday School teacher. I have to say that I really appreciate Johnny McCoy for bringing me on staff. God allowed him to see something that I, and others, never could have seen.

CHAPTER 2

Step Out In Faith

SEVERAL MONTHS LATER, (AUGUST, 1996) DEBBIE AND I WENT TO the Alaska Baptist Convention annual meeting. While we were there, God was working in my heart and I turned to Debbie saying, "We need to talk. I have something I need to tell you." She looked puzzled and asked, "What?" I told her we needed to go home early because God wanted me to resign. She smiled and said, "God already told me."

As we talked, I expressed that I knew God wanted me in full time ministry. Our direction from the Lord was much like that of Abraham. The only place we could feel him moving us was south. We felt, as though once we moved "south", He would direct us from there. I asked the Lord for a verse that would relay to fellow pastors and friends that we had to move, whether or not we had a church or a place to call home. I kept this request of God to myself. The next morning, Debbie got up and said that she had a dream with a scripture attached. She got her Bible and read to me, Joshua 3:15-16, "Now the Jordan is at flood stage during harvest. Yet as soon as the priests who carried the ark reached the Jordan, and their feet touched the water's edge, the water from upstream stopped flowing. It piled up in a heap a great distance away…" (NIV) Here was my answer with scripture to back it up! We needed to step out in faith, put our feet "in the water" so to speak, by moving south, and the Lord would show us where to go from there.

We returned to North Pole that August day, and I submitted my resignation to be effective October 1, 1996. Some things had to happen before we could leave the area.

Our business had not gone well while I was working part time for the church. In the previous six months the business had lost tens of thousands of dollars. I cried out to the Lord! "Lord, I am finally where you want me to be, so why are we losing so much money?" A voice, as clear as any I have ever heard said, "I never told you to go into this business." He was right; of course, I had never talked to Him, asked Him, or even prayed about it. I admitted, "Lord I never sought your will for me or searched out your plan for my life in this." I prayed, "Ok Lord, what do You want me to do?" God told me to get out of the business, but not to sell it. We did sell the inventory and we were still over six hundred thousand dollars in debt. We had a ten-year lease we had just signed the year before. The lease was four thousand, two hundred and fifty dollars ($4,250.) a month. In addition we had two houses and a lot of other things, including a business debt of one hundred thousand dollars at ten per cent interest based only on a contractual handshake. We had only begun to pay it off at one thousand one hundred eighty dollars ($1,180.) a month. Whatever God was doing, it was going to have to be miraculous.

In pursuing this new course God had set before us, we decided to sell everything we could. We put our houses on the market and the realtor told us that it would be months before they would sell, if then. We had earnest money on both of them within one week. We liquidated the houses, the inventory, and any and everything else we could. I even sold my truck so we would have enough money to live on until Christmas of 1996. Loading a U-Haul with what was left, which was basically household furniture and a car, my wife and I and our three youngest children headed for Anchorage. We rented a small three-bedroom apartment, unloaded everything that would fit and stored the rest.

Debbie had been silently praying, asking God, as confirmation of His call, to give me a place to preach every Sunday. On the first Monday of October, I called the Alaska Baptist Convention office and mentioned I would be glad to supply preach while in Anchorage. By Wednesday, I was booked every Sunday for two months. I was once again surprised by the power of my wife's prayers!

I didn't know Pastor Bill Branch, of North Kenai Baptist Church in Nikiski was at the same convention in August. I knew what he looked like but I really didn't know him. He had left the meeting early to go to Nikiski and resign the church and retire. His resignation was effective October first. We were five hundred and fifty miles apart and God was working in our hearts at the same time. Over the years God has blessed us so many times by revealing instances such as these to us.

CHAPTER 3

Put Your Foot In The Water

TWO DAYS AFTER ARRIVING IN ANCHORAGE, I RECEIVED A CALL from Jim Wolverton, a member of North Kenai Baptist Church in Nikiski. He had been told that I was willing to fill the pulpits in our Baptist churches. He said they needed someone to preach. I told him I had only one free Sunday in October, which happened to be the exact date he was requesting: October 13th. Nothing in this whole situation was a surprise to God. Only He can make the puzzle pieces of our lives fit together to create the masterpiece that He desires.

Prior to our move and prior to the closing of our business we had made a commitment we needed to honor. I was to participate as one of the auctioneers at an auction in Fairbanks over a three-day period, October 10, 11 & 12th. We finished on Saturday evening late and flew back to Anchorage early on Sunday morning. At one in the morning, we arrived in blizzard conditions and, if I remember correctly, Anchorage received over twenty inches of snow in a twenty-four hour period that day.

I usually took Debbie and the girls with me when I went to preach, but I didn't know if we would be back in time for school on Monday and it was time for mid-term exams. So they stayed home. Little did we realize school would be cancelled on Monday due to the amount of snowfall. A case of us not trusting that the Lord had this whole plan under control.

Debbie had been to Nikiski as a teenager and had not been impressed, but I had never been there. Leaving at five in the morning, I started the 175-mile drive to Nikiski. I thought I would arrive in time for Sunday school with time to spare. I drove a hundred miles without seeing any cars and pushed snow with my bumper most of the way. I couldn't believe the roads. Nothing had been plowed the entire distance and there were no tracks from other vehicles. I couldn't turn around because I couldn't see the sides of the road. When I arrived in Kenai it was snowing so hard I couldn't see any buildings -- only a few lights and a few signs along the way. Finally coming up on a service station, I pulled in and went to the outside phone. I made a collect call home. Debbie answered and asked me where I was. I told her I didn't know. I knew I must be close to Nikiski, but I had no idea where the church was. She had a lady (Vicki Hensley) from the church on call waiting and was able to ask her for directions. I told Debbie I was at a Seven-Eleven store. Vicki told her to relay to me to continue on the road I was on because I was only a few miles away.

It was 11:15 a.m. when this tired preacher arrived. I went to the front of the church to wait until it was time to preach. There were only about thirteen people there due to the blizzard. After the service, JR and Vicki Hensley took me out to lunch. Another lady, Vickie Fain, joined us. We went to eat at the only restaurant in Nikiski and we were the only ones there. They started to ask me all kinds of questions. Finally it dawned on me they didn't have a pastor and this was quickly becoming an impromptu interview. I asked them how long they had been without a pastor. They answered two weeks. I found it amusing that they were looking so quickly. When they began to question me, I thought I should take care of this fast. I gave them a long list of the things that were wrong with me. I didn't have the right education, divorce was in my past, retired military, little formal education, and right on down the list, but it didn't seem to faze them at all.

After lunch I went to JR and Vicki's home a few miles down the road. When we arrived I asked if there was a place where I could lie down and rest. They led me to a downstairs bedroom to rest, pray, and go over my sermon for that night. I didn't know they were upstairs calling people, trying to get them to come to the evening service. That night, at church, there were twenty-five to thirty people who braved the weather.

As I sat on the front pew waiting to preach, I knew God was calling me to this church. In the past twenty-four hours I had been lost, cold, tired, and lonely, but in that moment God brought clarity, energy, and the warmth of his peace that this was where I was to be. "Alright, Lord," I said, "I am convinced. Now, you have to convince them!".

I preached the message, and following the service all the people went downstairs to the fellowship hall for coffee. I assumed this was a normal thing. I needed to get back on the road and although the snow had stopped, my car was covered from sitting outside all day. As I began cleaning it off, every few minutes someone would come out to talk with me. Several asked me if I would consider coming as pastor. I said "yes". Then I would go back to cleaning my car. Another one would come out, ask a few questions, and then go back inside. They asked me if I had a resume. I said "yes" and they asked me to send them one.

I later found out the church members didn't usually go down to the fellowship hall for coffee. However, as God would have it, while I was scraping snow from my car, they were discussing the possibility that God could be leading them to ask me to be their new pastor. I finally started home and in Soldotna on an "s" curve called Pickle Hill, a man lost control of his car and he sideswiped me. The car was damaged all down one side and the other driver didn't have insurance. Neither of us had a cell phone to call the police, so we just went our own ways. My thought was, "You know, Lord, you are doing such a great and mighty work that I'm not going to let anything distract me from it." I did realize, however, that I had another potential problem.

Debbie and I have argued very little in our marriage, but we have had a few loud discussions. One of those discussions was about uprooting the girls again. They were in a Christian school and doing very well. Debbie wanted to keep them there regardless of where we served and I made the comment I would never consider a church outside of the Anchorage Bowl. You should never say "never". Crying out to God, I asked, "Lord how am I going to tell Debbie? I have just told her I wouldn't take a church outside of the Anchorage area. Show me what to tell her. Father I don't know what to say." I was literally crying and hanging on to the wheel for the whole four hour trip.

CHAPTER 4

Lord, What Am I Going To Tell Debbie?

WHEN I GOT HOME, I WALKED UP TO THAT LITTLE apartment and opened the door. I went to the bedroom and before I could say a word, Debbie said, "I know, you don't have to tell me. God told me where we are supposed to go…North Kenai Baptist Church." I told her I didn't know how to tell her and I was so glad God did. She looked at me and said, "But Denver there is nothing there." She even went on to say there was very little in Soldotna or even Kenai when she had visited in 1976. I told her I had seen street lamps, but I couldn't see the buildings because of the snow. There had been lights indicating life. There had to be a city there.

Debbie's parents lived in Anchorage at that time. We asked them if they would pick the girls up from school on Tuesday so we could drive to Nikiski and not be rushed. When they left for school, Deb and I set out to see what was in the area. The weather had cleared and the snowplows had been busy clearing the roads.

I had only been to two places. One was the church so we drove there. We parked in the parking lot and looked around and prayed together, asking God for His direction. Debbie has a gift of seeing things that others don't see. She looked at me and said, "Denver, this looks like the church in Peretti's book, *"This Present Darkness"*. I can see a cloud over this church." I asked her, "Do you mean we are not supposed to come here?" She said, "No, I think we're supposed to be here, but this is not going to be easy. There is a spiritual battle going on here.

We drove to JR and Vicki's house, which was the only other place I knew in the area. We didn't know what to expect, but then we didn't know JR and Vicki. They were as friendly as could be. We have been friends for over twelve years, and now you can't keep Vicki quiet. JR is a man with more integrity than almost anyone I know, and it shows in his life. They welcomed us in and while we were sitting there visiting, the phone rang. Vicki answered, and listened for a bit and then said, "Well, you will never guess who is here!" It led me to believe that they were talking about us. It was Vickie Fain, the lady who had gone to lunch with us on Sunday. In ten to fifteen minutes, there was a knock on the door, and in walked Vickie with her husband, Terry. We talked for a while, and then they started asking questions. They even had a few questions for Debbie.

We arrived back in Anchorage that evening to a message on our answering machine. The church wanted us to come to a Friday night social. Every October they held a "Hobo Party". They asked us to come as a family, so we did. It was kind of unusual to meet a bunch of people, outside, around a campfire with everyone eating soup out of tin cans. People were dressed as hobos, faces painted, clothes ripped, enjoying each other's company, and having a great time. As they talked, they spoke honestly about their church, the community, and their lives. Some shared their life stories in an attempt to gauge our "shock" to certain life situations. We were not hindered, we had ministered to many people with "pasts" and realize that God forgives and is merciful.

Again, we returned home to a message on our answering machine. This time it was Jim Wolverton, chairman of the Pastor's Search Committee, asking that we come back in view of a call as pastor on

November 17, 1996. I phoned him back and told him we would be honored to.

On that Saturday, the pastor search committee questioned us. They asked all the questions that most candidates are asked. I told the girls they would most likely ask them questions also and they were to answer all of the questions, as long as they were truthful. One of our daughters, Jeanette, (a fifth grader at the time), did not want to leave Anchorage and move from the beginning. As the committee asked her what she thought of moving to Nikiski, she shared openly. She said she hated Nikiski and didn't want to live there. As we drove by the oil refineries, she said they would poison all of us. The ironic thing is that she now lives in Kenai and is married and has a son three years old and a baby a year old. Jesse, her husband, works at one of the oil refineries, and they will probably never leave, unless God leads them. It is amazing how God changes people over time. He has the plan for our lives and knows what is best.

I remember that Sunday evening very well. There was a group of about thirty-three people who could vote. There was another group who were curious. Our family went downstairs during the vote. I told Debbie "I have never gone to a church without a one hundred percent vote. I don't know what to do if it is not a hundred percent. How much are we willing to battle the people who vote against us?" During those moments, we earnestly prayed about this. I will never forget when Terry Fain, chairman of the deacons, came downstairs. He showed me the vote tally and out of thirty-three votes there were thirty-three yes—100%! We had never talked about salary or salary package. He showed me the package available. I believe it was something around thirty-three thousand per year. I could divide it up anyway I chose to: health insurance, car allowance, salary, annuity, etc., but that was it-- $33,000 flat. There was no such thing as "benefits". I had not even looked at the budget. I probably should have. I told Debbie our salary was probably more than the church could afford. I was right. They extended a call for us to come and we accepted. Our first Sunday was December 20, 1996.

CHAPTER 5

God Forgives Can You?

EARLIER I SPOKE ABOUT A TRAGIC EVENT, WHICH CAUSED ME to be out of the ministry for three and a half years.

I went through a divorce.

Afterward, during that three and a half year period, I fell in love with a wonderful young lady, Debbie Hanniford. Her husband had passed away, and she was raising three little girls alone. Debbie's father was a deacon in one of the churches I had pastored. We were married, on December 29, 1992. God has blessed me so much that I can hardly stand it. At times I have felt like Job, even though I lost a lot, God has given back ten fold of the things I lost.

My life with Deb and our kids has been a good one. At the time we married, I was not in the pastorate. Growing up, I had come to believe that divorce ended all possibilities of service for the Lord. God periodically would quicken my heart toward possibilities, but I would argue with Him, which is a foolish thing to do. In March of 1995, after struggling with this burden, I finally gave it all over to God; I knew I had been forgiven. I was filled with His Spirit, and I can't even describe the cleansing and healing that went on in my heart. God began to show me that He could use me again. He revealed to me that my calling had not changed, though my circumstances had.

That same year, my friend, Johnny McCoy and I went with some other clergy to a Promise Keepers Conference in Atlanta, Georgia. At that conference, God did a deep work in my heart. I remember staying awake most of the night, crying and praying. My tears soaked my pillow. As I was praying, God revealed to me that I needed to give my testimony before our church. In my heart I said, "God I have never asked anyone to let me preach, and I don't want to now. You are going to have to provide an opportunity for me." The very next morning, the first thing Johnny said to me was, "Denver, I would really like for you to preach the Sunday night after we get back."

The Sunday night after we returned, a snowstorm cancelled the evening service. However, the following Sunday night, I was to give my testimony. I knew God was leading me in a new direction. Before that service, I was in an upstairs bathroom, making sure my hair was combed and I was presentable. When I came out I met an old friend, Marlin Starnes and his wife, Neva. I have known Marlin most of my life. He was pastor of a camp in Missouri that I had attended as a teenager. He was also the pastor of Emmanuel Baptist Church just outside of De Soto, Missouri. We have some history.

I also knew how Marlin felt about divorce. We had talked a lot about a lot of things. Upon seeing him I asked God, "Why is Marlin here? Him of all people!" It really threw me for a loop. But I had told the Lord I was committed to doing what He told me to do. I preached that night and gave my testimony. At the end of the service, Marlin made a beeline to where I was standing. I was scared. He grabbed me and said, "I am so glad God is going to use you, again."

Marlin had not been to the church at all since we had been there, and he had not known I would be preaching that night. God orchestrated these events from the very beginning. He knew all along Marlin would be there to hear and see the miraculous work God was doing in my life.

That is the way God works in the lives of His children. He is sufficient for their every need. All of us need to realize that God has a customized plan for each of us and His plans are good and involve a future and a hope. All who are called by the name of Christ have these promises.

CHAPTER 6

God Sent A Predecessor

At the time of Brother Bill Branch's retirement from North Kenai Baptist Church, the church body called Brother Marlin Starnes to act as interim pastor and help them with the task of calling a new pastor.

It was exciting to me to find that God was not finished with me and had sent Brother Marlin that snowy night to hear my testimony. Had he not heard the testimony, he may have steered the church away from choosing me as their pastor. Brother Marlin knew me and the fact I wanted to serve the Lord and he guided them in that decision.

I recall he told several people I was on fire for the Lord, and not to pour cold water on me, but to listen to what God had to say through me. He cautioned them not to harden their hearts, but to open their hearts and follow God's direction.

It is easy for us to travel down life's road and forget God is sovereign and in control of our lives and circumstances. Somehow if we could daily remember this, we would have less worry and concern in our lives. God used the circumstances of a sermon, and an interim time to confirm His will and His plan for a family, a church body, and a community.

CHAPTER 7

Problems? Not Here

I PREACHED AT NORTH KENAI BAPTIST CHURCH ON OCTOBER 13, 1996 and began as pastor on December 20, 1996. During the weeks between October 13th and December 20th, God opened the door for me to learn about the North Kenai Baptist congregation. God allowed us to get acquainted with and spend time with Frankie and Retha Hall. Frankie had a brain tumor and had to have treatments in Anchorage. It was difficult for him to get transportation back and forth to the airport so we volunteered to pick him up at the airport in Anchorage and take him to the hospital on Mondays. Then on Fridays we would pick him up at the hospital and take him to the airport so he could fly back to Kenai. I also visited him each Wednesday in the hospital. I saw him about every other day.

Something the church members didn't know (but I guess they will now) is that Frankie filled me in on the history of the church and the church members. Now Frankie was a very vocal person and he told me a lot of things. He and his wife had been there from the very start. As I arrived at the church as pastor, I felt as though I was already familiar with people through my conversations with Frankie, even though I only had his point of view. I was aware of the past, so nothing came as a surprise. I didn't even have to pry. God used these times to teach me about the area, alert me to some situations, and prepare me to lead the church. Frankie passed away our first week at the church and I was honored to preach his funeral on my first Sunday in Nikiski. Retha is still a member and has been active all through the years in the ministry of the church.

At North Kenai, we spent three weeks just worshipping before I assumed the role of pastor. Brother Marlin Starnes, the interim pastor, preached and we were able to simply worship. Brother Marlin mentioned to me he had never been in a situation quite like this one; nor had I. He said there were times he didn't get into the pulpit until eleven forty-five, and the people wanted to be out by twelve. It was not only the long song service, but the prayer time seemed to dominate the service. (There is nothing wrong with long prayer, but this was not the time to "catch up" on private prayer for the week.) Each time someone took the podium, it took several minutes to switch.

The church had a Worship Committee and I asked to meet with them the first Sunday night. I gave them some ideas to consider. One was about the time allotted to prayer time. I suggested taking a few prayer requests and then praying a brief prayer, asking God to bless the requests and to bless the services. The Prayer Chairman was willing to do this.

I had also noticed the awkwardness of the offering time, which could take as long as five or six minutes. As the plate was passed, I noticed there were people that didn't have any money and they seemed embarrassed that they did not have an offering. I really thought about this and prayed about it. I understand people need to worship God with singing and in tithes and offerings. I was also aware of some churches that had moved their offering time to the end of the worship service. I first asked the committee to try a box in the back of the auditorium, and see if that might help. There were some objections to that, so I asked them to try it for ninety days and see what God could do. Even though most of the things I asked were to be on a ninety-day trial basis, nothing has gone back to the way it was before.

Offerings increased by using the boxes in the back. At the end of the service I always reminded people to give their tithes and offerings.

The first box was a wooden breadbox with a slit cut in it, which we sat on a table in the back of the sanctuary. Today there are two metal boxes mounted on the wall just outside the sanctuary.

CHAPTER 8

Sing A New Song

SEVERAL THINGS WE DISCUSSED AT THAT FIRST MEETING HAVE GREATLY impacted the church. I will be discussing more of these as we go.

One of the major transitions was going from traditional music to contemporary. I was very proud of our church. We were singing three hymns and then three choruses, having prayer time, and I was getting into the pulpit by eleven thirty. We were able to do all of this and still dismiss by twelve fifteen.

One day I was talking with another pastor, Jim Van Buskirk, pastor of a non-denominational church. We were kidding around and said we ought to switch pulpits one Sunday. We didn't tell the people, but on Sunday after Sunday School, I drove to his church, North Kenai Chapel and he drove to ours. We met Monday for lunch, and I told him how well his church was doing, and how God was working. I was raised with southern gospel music, and I really love the old hymns and I admitted that I really didn't know any of the songs they sang at his church. We talked about the differences in our services. We had a blended service at North Kenai Baptist and I asked him if he noticed. He said something then that really pierced my heart. He said their congregation had sung those choruses thirty years ago. In my heart I asked God to forgive me, for I thought as a church we were on the cutting edge, only to realize that we were singing choruses from thirty years ago. Jim was right. I could remember singing them when I was a teenager back in the 60's and 70's.

I asked God what He wanted me to do. I prayed and asked God to give me wisdom. My mom was the spiritual leader in our home and she always stressed praying for wisdom. I have done so ever since I can remember and it works. I tell some people this and they look at me oddly. If you think I lack wisdom now, just think what I would be like if I didn't pray for it!

I asked God to show me a vision of what needed to be done. I started praying for guidance, and a few months later I talked with Vicki Hensley, our worship leader about learning some new choruses. I wanted to change some things around, such as using some of the newer songs in our services. So we began to learn new choruses. It wasn't long until we were singing more choruses than we were hymns.

By about 1998, I went to the Christian bookstore in Kenai, Alaska. It was equipped with headsets for listening to music by different groups. I don't listen to music much; I don't even turn on the radio in the car. I usually use that time to talk to the Lord. As I indicated, my background is in southern gospel and I was not up on the new music. I put on the headset, and I asked God to show me the way. "Show me what you would have our church to do. What would be good for us?" I pushed every button on the machine, and I wrote down the names of groups that I was drawn to. After I had several of these written down, I went back to listen to the songs, and I prayed over each one. I really needed God's guidance. We wanted our church to be what God wanted it to be. If we were going to change the music, I really needed God's direction.

I finally realized that all of the songs I picked were from one group, called "Hillsong". This group is from Australia. I was blessed by their music and I purchased what I thought we needed to get started. Vicki and Deb got together to learn the songs. It was a stretching experience for both of them. They really had to work together to make this happen. The worship team struggled with the "mechanics" of singing the new music. Eventually, however, the words penetrated their hearts and they began to truly lead in worship. I set a date of the first of January to begin the new music program. We began to sing along with the CD soundtracks.

Vicki had always said that if God would provide a man who could lead music, she would gladly step down. I always thought she was joking. Vicki started having trouble with her voice and went to the doctor who told her not to talk for four to six weeks. God had already placed someone in our midst to supply our need.

When we built the addition in 1999, a one-bedroom studio apartment was built in with the hopes that it would house a youth minister one day. The Lord brought Gaylon Moss, from North Carolina to bring about His will for our church. Gaylon was on the Peninsula conducting Disaster Relief training. Upon completion of the training, he requested a tour of our church to see all that had been built by work teams. As he was walking through the new addition, he inquired about the apartment. I explained that it was to be home to a youth minister one day. It was nearly a year later he contacted me and said that he knew a man who would be perfect for the ministry here. When he arrived home, he began speaking with Corey McGee, telling him about the work in Nikiski. I contacted Corey within a few days and we began spending several hours on the phone sharing the vision God had given each of us.

In September, 2001, the church called Corey McGee as Youth Pastor. To our surprise, Corey had been a worship leader in a year round camp in New Mexico, just outside of Capitan. When Corey came and began working with our youth, we learned that he had musical ability. He played the guitar and sang. So, Corey began leading the worship service during Vicki's absence. At the end of that time, I asked Vicki if she was ready to go back to work. She told me she felt Corey should lead the music and he has been doing so ever since. Corey brought with him some of the songs we had been singing. I even recognized some of the titles when I saw them on the screen. Most of the songs had come from the "WOW" cds. The only musician we had then was Corey on the guitar.

Corey served as Youth Pastor for several years and then became Associate Pastor of Music and Youth. In 2007, he married Ashley Samora, a talented young lady who, with her family is a charter member of the church. God not only brought him to Nikiski to serve faithfully but to provide his helpmate. They now have a two-year-old son.

In the summer of 2003, we had a group coming for special services and they asked if we had a set of drums. When we said we didn't, they asked if they purchased them to use while they were here if we would use them when they left. I said, "yes!" even though we didn't have anyone to play them. Again, God was already at work. A young man had started attending our church with his little family. A few weeks after they began attending the church, my wife observed him during the service patting the back of the pew in time to the music as if he were playing the drums. One Sunday during the welcome time she asked him if he played an instrument. He looked at her kind of funny and said, "Yes, the drums". This was our first real introduction to Randy Lewis. I talked to Randy and told him we were getting a new set of drums and that Debbie told me he played. I ask him if he would be interested in playing them for us. At first, he was non-committal.

I took the van and picked up the drums and the first place I went was to Randy's house. I asked him if he would come help set them up. We got them set up and tuned and he really seemed to enjoy playing them. I told him that the Worship Team got together about nine to nine thirty on Sunday morning to go over the music they were going to use. I asked if he would be interested in taking part. He told me he wasn't interested in playing in church because he felt a person on the platform needed to be right with the Lord. At that point he felt like he wasn't right with God. I informed him he didn't have to play for church; it was just a practice session. He came and practiced with the praise team. It was the maiden voyage for the drums he went ahead and played for the service. God's conviction was heavy upon him and within a week he rededicated his life to the Lord and has played ever since.

God began to work in the Lewis family and in 2003 Randy quit his job as a carpenter and came to work at the church supported only by love gifts. With a family of eight, this was quite a step of faith for Randy and his wife Destiny. Randy joined our staff as Minister of Children and Facilities in 2004.

Another drummer now plays part of the time and a bass guitarist plays regularly. Debbie played the piano and the church has a keyboard that is played when someone is present with the ability. We lost some people due to the change of the style of our music and worship. One couple was very vocal about their dislike of the music and they left to attend a more traditional church. We had others who didn't like the music but they stayed anyway

I don't know anyone who drives down the road and listens to the radio that likes all of the music they hear. Don't get me wrong -- I love the hymns. But people today want music that is lively. They want music they can sing along with. They want music that fits them. Music speaks to people and touches them in ways the spoken word cannot. I believe music is a vital part of bringing younger people into our churches. Children love to sing worship songs, and I love to hear them sing. Contemporary Christian music can replace the world's music because young people like it. We had thirty-five to fifty children, first through sixth grades, on any given Sunday. They participated in the worship service then after the singing they were dismissed to Junior Church.

Youth are willing to attend the services because they enjoy the music. They get involved with hand motions and singing. I challenged Corey every once in a while to throw in a new song. I didn't want us to get stuck in a rut. (A rut is a grave with both ends kicked out.) I didn't want us to be so hung up we become more interested in traditions than in souls. God, in His Word, says for us to sing a new song.

Rick Ferguson, my friend from Riverside Baptist Church in Denver Colorado, found a church bulletin that was one hundred years old. He said you could lay it beside the bulletin from his church and see nothing had changed. It brought conviction to his heart, and his church. Rick and I talked about this a lot in the short time we had together. He poured himself out at every revival, and he preached that you have to be willing to change and keep the "main thing the main thing.

Is it easy to go from traditional style of music to contemporary? No, not always! Yes, there are always some people who aren't going to like it. If the younger generation is to be reached, ideas about methods of worship and outreach have to be updated with the times. The secular, business world markets products to keep up with the times. Thirty years ago kids carried around a walk-man that would hold one cassette tape with approximately sixteen songs on it. Today's mp3 players can be as small as a credit card and hold as much information as a small computer! Times have changed and no one really wants to go back thirty years.

Change can be good and revitalizing. Although we make some changes to bring in the lost we <u>do not change the message</u>, only the method. I would not criticize any church that sings all hymns or has a blended service or prefers contemporary style. I would say to let the Lord lead you. We can't let people's personal tastes stand in the way of what God wants to do. Something I recently heard, but do not know who to give the credit, really spoke to my heart. It was: "We must be anchored to the Rock, but geared to the times."

CHAPTER 9

What Is Wrong With Us, Lord

AS WE BEGAN SETTLING IN TO LIFE AT THE CHURCH, I began to get a bit discouraged. We had been at the church for an entire year and seen only seen four "new" visitors come through the doors. There were folks who were previous attendee who came out of curiosity or because friends invited them back or told them the church was different, or those things that bring people back with a new pastor. Some stayed, others did not. As time went by I began to notice that we were not reaching any new, unsaved members of the community.

After many years of serving in churches where there was a strong military base, I began to question God as to how to bring people in. I had never been a part of a community like this. Although Nikiski was a very transient community, it was for different reasons than I was accustomed to. Military communities are full of people that are coming and going. Also, many of those are "churched", meaning they grew up in the "Bible Belt" and usually will find a church when they arrive at their new destination.

In Nikiski, people came and went, but mostly went. Many left to return to family in the "lower 48" or left due to the economy and to follow a job. There was a time of people leaving one church or another to attend a new church. I have never been a pastor who likes to change the fish in the fishbowl! A church needs to be built by reaching the unsaved and un-churched in its community.

As I stood in the sanctuary at the third window from the front, overlooking the road and our community, I asked the Lord, "How do we reach this community for You?" He impressed on my heart to go out and meet people where they are. Get involved with them and meet their needs. I really began to seek Him and be vigilant at watching and observing the needs of those living around our church.

CHAPTER 10

I Was Right After All

WHEN WE ACCEPTED THE CALL TO THE CHURCH I MENTIONED to Debbie it would be nice to have a 15- passenger van for the church to use. I felt sure the church would not be able to afford to purchase one. The church had given me a pay package I could divide any way I chose. We decided we could purchase the van; using it as our second vehicle and as a vital tool for the church. It was our hope and prayer it would be used to bring children in to the church and to use for youth activities and any other function when we needed to transport people.

After looking in Anchorage, we purchased a 1995 Ford, white 15-passenger van. We eagerly loaded it up and took our first load of household belongings to Nikiski the first weekend in December. Returning to Anchorage; after spending the day, we were driving on the dark, snow-covered road outside of Sterling. We rounded a curve and there in the middle of the road was a huge bull moose. There was no way to avoid hitting it and we slammed into him. The impact was like hitting a brick wall. I quickly made sure all of the girls and Debbie were ok. The first thing Deb asked was "Are you SURE we are supposed to be coming here?" I told her "Yes, all good things come from God and this is not a good thing. God must want to do something great in Nikiski because this is the second accident trying to deter us!" The newspaper stated the new pastor in Nikiski was already feeding the hungry. Alaska has a road kill program and the moose was salvaged for the needy.

The van was just a few hundred dollars from being totaled in the accident, but was repaired and served many years afterward as faithful transportation not only for our family, but for the church also. Over time, we put approximately one hundred and eighty-nine thousand miles on it. When we paid it off, we sold it to the church for thirty-five hundred dollars.

I was correct when I suspected the church did not have the income to pay me what they had stated they had offered. After several months, I spoke with them and agreed to take no more than half of what came in up to the salary package. If the entire amount did not come in during the month, Vicki, the treasurer, would keep track of the deficit and make up the difference to me when they were able. We operated this way for approximately three years.

During this time, God provided our needs and we saw him do many wonders. The church has been meeting the budget now for several years as God has blessed.

CHAPTER 11

Open Our Eyes, Lord

WHEN I FIRST ARRIVED AT THE CHURCH EVERY ONE SAID we had a food pantry. I was the only employee of the church at that time. I looked all over the church and I could find nothing. In fact, we had a mouse that was starving to death!

Finally, I asked someone about the food ministry. I was told when someone called about food they would be told about the Kenai Food Bank. Folks who were in need of the food could go to the food bank and charge the amount of their purchase to the church. The church would then pay the bill. My reaction was, "is that really a hands on ministry?" I was the only one at the church and calls for food were sporadic. I was curious about whom they were calling when they weren't calling our church. I took the van and went to the food bank to find out how this worked. I asked the lady in charge if I could just purchase the food and distribute it from our church. She indicated this was exactly how the program was designed to work.

So, I loaded up the fifteen-passenger van from the front seats to the back, as much as I could possibly fit in. At that time they charged ten cents per pound of food. I paid for it and brought it back to the church. I added to the few shelves we had. I lined the food up in a hallway that was used for storage. Our members assumed that those in need would not come to the church for food because no one had ever done it before. They wouldn't even know it was here, I was told. This was the birth of our food pantry.

The first week our food pantry was operational, three individuals came to inquire about food! They had never come before! God led them to the church building! During the next eight years, we distributed over a hundred boxes of food per year. A box would feed a family for one or two weeks. It still amazes me how God can work!

God used this food pantry in the "early days" to be instrumental in beginning our van ministry. As we were looking to reach people outside the church and they would call for food, I would tell them I would deliver it to their house. I would inquire as to how many were in the family, how many were children, and how many adults. Then I would get a box of food and I would add or take away whatever was needed to fit that family. I would put it in the van and deliver it. It grabs a person's attention when someone brings food personally to their house. I knocked at the door and when they answered it, I would ask if I could bring in the food. I would always ask if there was anything else we could do for the family. Once inside I would look around to understand their living conditions. It helped me get an idea of how we could minister in other ways. If they had children, I would ask if we could pick them up for Sunday school. Debbie drove the van for the first eighteen months picking up people in the community for church. As time passed, Jim Wolverton began driving the van. As a matter of fact, he drove the van or bus for the church for over nine years until he went home to be with the Lord in November of 2008.

When we started visiting homes asking kids to ride the bus, there were some people who would say, "My kids can go, but I don't want to wake up to get them ready". I know it is hard to believe, but one or two of the ladies of our church would go to the home on Sunday morning and get the kids up and dressed. They would put them either in their vehicle or the van and bring them to church. Once they were at the church, we fed them breakfast.

One van, nearly demolished by a moose, was the start of this ministry and because of it, over one hundred kids came to know the Lord and were baptized! Praise Him for allowing us this van.

In 1999, we were able to purchase another van. We used these vans on weekdays for work teams who would come to Nikiski to help with our buildings and Vacation Bible Schools during the summer. On Sunday the vans were used to bring boys and girls to Sunday school. One lady came up to Nikiski from the "lower 48" for several months exclusively to help with the van ministry. She was a blessing!

Most of our ministries started this way. A need would arise and we would try to figure out how to meet it. When we started the van ministry, it wasn't in the budget. We would just in faith figure out a way to get the gas money, insurance, and other needed things. God blessed and our vehicle fleet grew.

CHAPTER 12

No Fishing In The Parking Lot

ABOUT SIX OR SEVEN YEARS AGO I PREACHED A SERMON titled "No Fishing In The Parking Lot". I told about people who go out and buy the best equipment: the best fishing pole, the best lures, even the best boat, everything they needed to fish with. How foolish it would be then to sit in the parking lot and try to catch fish. Of course, there are no fish in the parking lot. If they never took that boat out in the water, they would never catch fish. God's Word talks a lot about being fishers of men. He gave illustrations of where to put our nets.

The next Sunday when I came to church there was a sign in the sanctuary that said "No Fishing In The Parking Lot". That is what the core of our church was all about. Fishing for men can only take place where the "men" are. People aren't storming the doors of the church trying to get in, but people outside the doors have important needs. God tells us to feed the hungry, to clothe the poor, and give water to the thirsty. He says when we do it for the least; we are doing it for Him.

Folks, we are doing ministry for Jesus, we don't do feeding, clothing, ministering because we like it. We don't do these ministries for show. We do it for the Lord. We reach out into the community so we can earn the right to tell them about Jesus. We don't try to knock them over the head and tell them about Jesus; we meet their needs. When their needs are met, we are able to tell them about how much God loves them. Do they all come to Christ? No, but I know of no other program where every one comes to know Him. We don't know in advance who will accept Him and who won't. But, when you start meeting their needs possibly someone else will come to the Lord because you met the need of someone they know.

We don't catch every fish in the ocean, but when we start fishing we will catch some. Ask God to open your eyes to the needs of people around you. Drive through an area and pray for those people. Maybe it's an area that most people avoid, but these residents are still souls and loved in God's sight. Get a heart for people, pray for them, and ask God what He wants you to do about them. Ask God to show you what your church can do.

People are watching you to see if you and your ministries are real. We did this kind of ministry for over ten years. People asked when we were going to burn out. I believe when you are doing ministry for the right reason and in the right way you may not burn out. If God calls you to a ministry, to reach the unsaved, He provides the strength and endurance. Every area is different, so, reach out to the people of your area. Look to see what you can do to meet their needs.

Reaching the community can sometimes expose problems in the church. Some members think, "If you bring in a bunch of "snotty nose" kids, they will make a lot of noise, or they will tear things up. They won't know how to act in church, or they will go through church like a whirlwind and our church will never be the same". DO NOT be like an animal marking territory. Remember we are in God's territory.

We need to understand everything in a church building can be replaced, but we can't replace a soul that slips into eternity without Christ. If we won't allow them into the church, what are the chances of them accepting the Lord? Some say soul winning is someone else's job. No, it isn't. It is the job God gave each of us as individuals to do. We are reminded of this in the Great Commission in Matthew

28. Others may say, "Well, let some other church do it." Why would we willingly miss all the blessings that come from obedience? Some say "our building is too nice, or we have always done it this way" and change is not an option. Maybe it is time to get out of the rut and ask God how He wants it done. (Remember, a rut is a grave with both ends knocked out).

Maybe it is time to accept that the church building is meaningless; it is temporal; it is replaceable. It's the people in the building who mean the most to God. If we are not reaching out to people, meeting their needs, and telling them about Christ then we are nothing more than a COUNTRY CLUB CHURCH. I don't want to be a part of a country club church. That sounds kind of cold and harsh to some people, but it is the truth. I want to be a part of a church that preaches the gospel and reaches out to meet the needs of people. I want people to grow in Christ and I know it can be done. I have seen it. Ministry can be done any place. All you need to do is ask God to show you, and then step out in faith believing.

Another point about fishing is not to fish in another person's fishing hole. You can have all the best equipment, but if you are just attempting to catch a fish from someone else's pond and release it in your pond, that is not healthy or ethical. Don't try to get people who attend other churches to switch to yours. All that happens then is a transfer of fish from one bowl to another. Try to get lost people into the fold. When they see your church is alive and thriving they will want to come. People want to be apart of a living organism, not a dead one. When you fish in another church's fishing hole, the unhappy, unhealthy, miserable fish, will move, but the problem within the person will manifest its self eventually in your church. People should only move to another church when they are absolutely sure God has placed them there. Any other reason will not stand the test of time. When we bring the un-churched person into the fellowship there are some things to realize. Un-churched people won't know their Bible. This will all be new to them. Many times we forget that if they have not been in church their whole life, they don't know who people are in the Bible or how to navigate the Bible. They are starting from ground zero. That person needs to feel comfortable to ask questions and get clarification. Many times they do not even understand our "churchy lingo". Talking down would never be good, but helping them understand is what God wants.

The reason the Lord left us on earth is to lead the lost to a saving knowledge of Him and teach the love of God to this world. Maybe it's time we understand what a lost person sees. We have had people come who are very open and they ask questions. They want to know why we do this or why we do that. Sometimes we have to ask ourselves why we do the things we do!

Look around your community and listen. Many folks told us they wouldn't be able to come to church because they didn't have good clothes to wear. For our area we felt it appropriate to dress differently to come to church. Suits and ties and nylons and dresses every Sunday went to the wayside. Comfort and allowing everyone to wear what they had and feel comfortable in God's house became our major priority. Your "neck of the woods" may not be like this, but listening to those you visit can give you a great insight as to how you can reach them in this way.

You may have the greatest visitation program in the world, but if people aren't coming to your church, it isn't working. I believe you have to work, to go out, and do ministry. I think it works effectively in small rural communities as well as in larger cities. You have to get out among people and give them a reason to come into the church.

CHAPTER 13

Changing Our World

IN LATE **1999**, I ATTENDED A MEETING IN ANCHORAGE AND following the meeting I joined the pastors at their weekly luncheon. Two of the men in attendance were Keith Loomis and Wade Henry. Keith was from World Changers; Wade was the Alaska World Changer contact. The discussion was about churches hosting World Changers a youth program of the North American Mission Board of the Southern Baptist Convention. World Changers takes young people and adults and involves them in hands-on ministry and in learning how to minister and what His calling could be for their lives. As I sat at this meeting and learned that World Changers is geared toward ministry to low-income, poorer communities where people are in dire need, I knew this was just what we needed in Nikiski. My first question was why don't we host them in Nikiski where the need is greatest.

The first year World Changers came to Alaska it was hosted in only Anchorage. That following year the ball began rolling and we hosted our first project in Nikiski in 2001. The following year projects were held in Anchorage, Wasilla, and Nikiski. Added to the Alaska projects over the past years, North Pole and Denali, Alaska. The Lord has allowed Nikiski to host projects each year since 2001. In alternating years Nikiski hosts two projects.

This was a great undertaking for a church of our size. There was much planning that went along with hosting these teams each year. There had to be places to sleep, shower, eat, and worship. Most of all there had to be funds to provide materials for the work on the homes.

Needy homeowners did not have the financial resources for the repairs on their homes.

The first year we hosted World Changers in Nikiski, living arrangements were made with Nikiski Jr./Sr. High School. The group was allowed to sleep and shower, and meals were served at the school. The second year we felt as though we could house the group at the church and utilize available funds a bit more effectively. Two weeks before World Changers were scheduled to arrive, we began moving everything out of each Sunday school classroom and the other rooms and offices of the church. Everything was placed in a storage area and room was made for bunk beds and space for guests. Work teams came to help our church prepare for this undertaking. Bunk beds were built so one person could sleep on the floor and two people slept on the bunk bed above him. The church was divided so males and females would not meet in the sleeping area.

The men of the church constructed a shower trailer from the ground up. It was made on wheels and axels so that in the event of a disaster, the trailer could be used and utilized for another need. It consisted of eight showers, with hot water on demand so that with eight showers running at the same time it would not run out of hot water. It was built with a 165k boiler and half-million BTU heat exchanger and two fifty (50) gallon hot water holding tanks. It was a work of art to the male population of the church! It was constructed so there were four showers on each half. The church building also had one shower in each of the restrooms and in the church office. The office building housed the summer staff. The shower trailer was moved up to the church building for easy access. A couple of years later, we were able to acquire another shower building where we also had washers and dryers. These showers were also used for World Changers and work teams.

We served meals for World Changers out of our kitchen in the church building. For the first couple of years I led the cooking teams and had several who assisted me with the task. After that the Lord brought Forrest Broussard (Bubba as he is known) back to Nikiski. He had owned and operated a local restaurant, but due to his health, he closed it. His cooking was and is well known in the Nikiski community. I asked him to help us cook for World Changers and he graciously accepted. Since that time, he has overseen the cooking for WC not only in Nikiski but also all over the state of Alaska. He also cooks for the church for Wednesday night meals and for any other meal that is served when he is in town. (When the snow flies, he becomes a snowbird, and goes to the Lower 48.) Several other people have given of their time and energy to serve in the meal programs of the church. I would list names, but fear I would leave someone out.

Volunteers at Lighthouse Community have always been unselfish and giving with their time and energy. Bubba has a great gift of recruiting all ages to assist in the kitchen. During the past several years Lighthouse youth have been second to none at helping, cleaning, carrying supplies, and doing any task requested. Bubba has taken several of the youth to the other World Changer locations to serve the Lord in the kitchen.

The first year we hosted World Changers, funds to complete the work on homes was an issue. We had people coming to do the work, but no money lined up to complete the task. Jim Wolverton was working at a local radio station and arranged for us to do a radio-a-thon. Some of the local Nikiski pastors and I went to the radio station and answered questions and calls and began raising funds from the Nikiski, Soldotna, and Kenai area. Local politicians also came and supported the cause by answering calls and questions. There was no doubt this area needed an organization like World Changers to come to our area and help local folks. During the radio-a-thon, twenty-four thousand ($24,000.00) was raised. I was elated and began putting together the list of homes, which would benefit most for a small amount of money. Most of the other Nikiski churches joined in by delivering lunches to work sites and other support needs. Seventeen homes were worked on that first year.

During the next year, I was at an annual World Changer retreat, and was approached by an individual who worked for Alaska Community Development Corporation in Palmer, Alaska. He was at this meeting as a financial agency representative. After hearing we had raised all of our funds the previous year, he told me there were funds available for exactly what we were doing. Since that time we worked through them and also through USDA Rural Development to obtain funds and discover homes that need repairs. The Lord joined us hand-in-hand to fulfill His purpose through World Changers in our area. We never lacked funds or houses to host the projects in our area and in our state. From the beginning of our alliance through 2008, we worked on over 300 homes on the Kenai Peninsula.

CHAPTER 14

Used Car Lot?

ABOUT THE THIRD YEAR WORLD CHANGERS CAME TO ALASKA, WE began to realize with the cost of vehicle rental it would be increasingly hard to sustain the program. At that time, and until the present, Jon Hodge was the World Changer, National Missionary for our geographic area. Jon and I were talking after one of our meetings and we began discussing the cost. Vehicle rental was going to cost approximately two hundred thousand dollars ($200,0000) for an eight (8) week period. We realized we didn't want anything to jeopardize World Changers coming to Alaska. I asked him what he would think if our church went to the bank and obtained a loan to purchase all the vehicles necessary to transport World Changers in the state. He supported the idea wholeheartedly.

This has been one of the most amazing ministries we have tackled. The number of vehicles we were able to acquire has amazed everyone. When we first purchased the vehicles and parked them on the land at the church, we heard comments such as, "Is this a used car lot? What are you doing with all those vehicles?" The door was then opened to share about what God was doing at the church through World Changers and the work teams. God can make anything a door if we just walk through it!

We began by acquiring a one hundred and fifty thousand dollar loan ($150,000) to purchase the vehicles to get started. Each year there would be a balloon payment of forty-thousand ($40,000.00) and we would make that payment by using the money that was appropriated for transportation by World Changer volunteers. By our church providing this ministry to them, World Changers was able to save approximately one hundred thousand dollars, ($100k), per year. Within four years, we paid off the loan. When we received the World Changer payment, we would pay our insurance for the year and see that any necessary maintenance was performed. We had a volunteer couple, Bob and Ruth Moreland, who would come to Nikiski so he could evaluate the vehicles thoroughly. Any problems arising during the summer usage months, he would correct. They were invaluable to this ministry. As a result of Lighthouse Community Church (LCC) making vehicles available for use by various work teams and World Changers, it provides a great savings and is a ministry to them. The vehicles are used year round in ministry when needed.

Many churches in the area and groups who came to Alaska for other ministry opportunities contacted LCC for use of the vehicles. We asked them to give a "love gift" of approximately a hundred ($100.00) per day to help offset the cost of maintenance. This service has saved them money from commercial rental and also helped the church with the funds necessary to keep the vehicles on the road.

Maintenance of the vehicles is expensive and must be done. Each of the vehicle costs approximately five hundred dollars ($500.00) per year to maintain and approximately five to six hundred dollars ($500 – $600.00) per year for liability only insurance. Additional expenses are gas, oil, and minor upkeep. Over the years, we obtained additional loans to refurbish the fleet of vehicles, purchase busses, and keep the vehicle ministry going. Each time a loan was arranged it was paid off in a timely manner. God blessed this ministry and through it we were also able to acquire land and a building that we would never have been able to purchase.

CHAPTER 15

Expand Our Territory

As we built the buildings we needed, it was becoming evident that we would be land-locked within a few years. There was a huge tract of land behind our property. I hoped we would be able to purchase some of it in the future. I knew there was no use in pursuing it at that point, as the church had no funds for it.

One day as I was at the office a gentleman walked in and informed me that the Federal Communications Commission (FCC) was purchasing the land I had my eye on. After a lengthy conversation I asked if they would be interested in selling just a small portion of the land to us or would lease us a portion of it for parking. He said the government does not sell land once they purchase it, after an hour and a half of talking about the government plan, he asked if we wouldn't just like to purchase a plot of it. I indicated yes we would, and wanted to say, "That's what I said in the beginning!" He asked how many acres we would be interested in. I stepped out and said, "10 acres". I knew we could not afford it but knew God had brought this man to my office. There was no reason he would have had to come and explain to me they were purchasing it. I also knew God would provide the means.

He said if we could get the land appraised and a survey done on it and close the sale at the same time the FCC did, we could purchase the ten acres. They were scheduled to close in approximately six weeks. I was ecstatic! I brought it before the church and they were also excited. I began contacting everyone who had been to the church and anyone I knew who could possibly help us. Following worship one morning, one of the couples in our church came to me and said they could help us out. They had just recently cashed in their retirements and were moving them around into a more profitable investment. They were willing to loan the funds to the church, but they would need to be repaid rather quickly. I accepted the offer and we proceeded on the land.

The way the Lord works is amazing! Our portion of the sale closed within six weeks and approximately six weeks before the government portion did, they closed at twelve weeks. Another instance of God being faster than the government!

Our vision for the community was that Lighthouse property would be the preferred "hang out" spot. We began clearing the ten acres that next spring. For approximately a month, every able-bodied man in the church operated the rented caterpillar and knocked down trees and cleared the land. We were getting the land ready for soccer fields, softball field, volleyball courts and picnic area. Since then, the community has used the field for soccer training, softball, paintball competitions, archery training, snow-machine riding, and other events.

One work team came the summer we were clearing the land. At that point we still owed $9,800 on the property. One of the members of that team asked me how much would it take to pay that land off and whom would he make the check to. I told him North Kenai Baptist. Before he left, he handed me a check in the amount of $10,000. and told me to pay off the land. I was able to give the money back to our church members in just a few short months since the day that man first entered my office.

Adjacent to the land that the fields are on was a parcel of six acres with a garage that would be perfect for a bus barn. We investigated and found we could obtain the land far more reasonably than we originally thought. We were able to use the vehicle fund and obtain a loan to purchase this land. I dreamed for several years that if this land could be purchased it would be a great spot for additional cabins. We saw the dream come true as we built five very simple 20' X 20'cabins in 2008. They could be used to house additional World Changers, for overnight camps for baseball and soccer and the fields can be utilized as well. In the event of overnight camps, we could hold services and really have some input in the lives of boys and girls. Overnight camps could help to bring in people from other parts of the state. These cabins could be used during May, June, July, and August, before freezing temperatures.

This additional land has provided a place for working on and maintaining the vehicles, as many as forty-nine cars, trucks, vans and busses, that God has provided and cabins for people who come and minister. The building is used as a garage for working on the vehicles. Also built in are three showers, and moved an additional shower trailer to the site. The residents of the cabins use these.

CHAPTER 16

Lookin' For A Mission Trip?

AFTER ALL OF THE YEARS OF HOSTING WORK TEAMS I have taken note of things that make them successful for both the church and visiting workers. If your group is interested in participating in a mission trip, here are some things you may want to consider

First, does the church that you are going to have the finances to purchase materials for the work they need done? Frequently, the smaller churches need work done, but don't have the finances. If they haven't had work teams before or for a long time, they may need a lot of incidental supplies. These could range from cooking utensils, to building tools, to children's ministry supplies. You may want to consider taking an offering before you leave your church to help finance purchase of the materials.

Second, ask about sleeping arrangements. How many rooms are available for sleeping? You may want to purchase air mattresses and leave them with your host church so other teams coming to work can use them. Contact the church to see what items you need to bring. By doing so, you will not waste needed luggage space by bringing unnecessary items.

Third, check on cooking arrangements. Inquire as to what the kitchen consists of, such as appliances, utensils, and things needed to cook meals for your group size. The church you are going to may not be set up for cooking all the meals your group will need. Be prepared to purchase some small kitchen utensils to use and then leave them when you go. You may consider supplying all of your food. Many smaller churches just don't have the means to supply all food for visiting work teams. If they are having multiple work teams in a summer, this would be impossible for them. You could offer to pay for the food and request that someone in the church do the shopping since a local person would know where the best prices would be. The best way to accomplish this is to make up a menu and a shopping list. This would insure there is enough food for everyone. Recruiting a cook for your trip is helpful. By bringing along one person to be responsible for meals many problems are eliminated.

Fourth, transportation is another major concern. If you fly into a more remote location, what form of ground transportation will you have? Many churches have vans that could be available for use. Speak with them about use of the vehicle. If the church is using it for a van ministry, the team may need to be flexible on Sundays or Wednesdays, while the church picks up children. Please remember to leave the vehicles clean of trash and with a full gas tank. The extra cost of fuel could cripple a small church. Remember, you may not be their only work team that summer.

Finally, leaving the church in a better position to minister when you leave than it was when you arrived is a great gift to that small congregation. Ask them what some of their needs are. Sunday school classes from your home church may be able to provide those needs. Ask what kind of ministries they are planning to start. Is there a way to help them get started in that ministry? Does your church have ideas, programs, supplies, equipment, or money to help support this church in becoming all God wants her to be? Offer to help with some local ministries, such as backyard Bible clubs. They may only need a little encouragement to help them get started, get a vision, and have the courage to step out. When they see what God is doing, they become more willing to keep stepping out.

Besides the above church-related considerations, a team should also think about these things:

1. When considering a mission trip, research the area. Surf the internet to find out what kind of community you are going to. By going online, you can find out what there is to do around that area. It is also a great way to find out about the economy of the area. That helps you get an idea of some ministries that may be needed.

2. Find a way to help the church minister to the community with little things, possibly a food program. We used a food ministry to start a van ministry. There are many avenues you can use to help out smaller churches. Repairing buildings or vehicles may be your main ministry focus, but you can find a way to minister to the people at the same time. You may be able to conduct a day camp for children in the area, while some are working on homes or buildings. Other ideas could be backyard Bible clubs or sports camps. When you meet the children in the area, you will know how to meet their needs. Those buildings you build and repair will need repair again in time, but the investment for the Lord in the lives of the people will be of eternal value. Many times the ministry you perform becomes a permanent ministry for the church.

3. Take the tools you are going to need with you. Many churches don't have tools or money to buy them. I know from experience that often a pastor will go into debt so teams will have all they need. Do not put that load on a pastor. Bring these tools and leave them if possible. We benefitted from the work of a lot of good churches, but two churches that greatly impacted LCC, are Mud Creek Baptist Church from North Carolina and Brushy Creek Baptist Church from South Carolina. They brought all their supplies, tools, and then paid for all they did. When they left, they left generous amounts of supplies behind. They gave us the leftover food, supplies, and other things. We

were blessed that they left the church much better off than it was when they arrived.

4. Ask God to show you what He desires; how He sees you reaching the community you are interested in going to. Look at what other churches are doing when they go on mission. Some of these ideas can be implemented in your mission trip if the Lord leads. It is important that nothing is done that might have a negative effect on the church.

5. One of the most important factors with a group is its attitude. Through the years we had a lot of experience with both good and bad attitudes and how they affected the project. We had over seventy-five work teams at our church, and only a couple of teams had an attitude problem. Attitudes should be right. It is hard to say you are serving the Lord when you are complaining and fussing all the time. Try not to have any expectations. Flexibility is the key! Expect the worst and praise the Lord when it turns out better. You should give God the glory when things go right and praise Him when they don't.

6. When you have the right attitude, and it is bathed in prayer, things will go a lot better, and if they don't, at least your attitude will not make it worse. Don't forget that your negativity may hurt the church you are trying to minister to. They have attempted to provide the very best for you and are excited you are there and are thankful for your help. As soon as you find out where you are going, start praying and give it over to God.

7. If you bring more people to work on a church than they have in the congregation, chances are you will overload their system. There may not be enough sleeping space, cafeteria space, or shower facilities. Many churches do not have shower facilities. You may need to find a local place that will let you use their showers. Some churches may not have a kitchen. You might have to eat out or adjust your group to fit

the size of the church. The size of your group shouldn't be larger than the church can handle.

It is a good idea to send one person to scout out the job site ahead of time to see how many people it will take to do the job. That person will be able to give the mission team ideas of what they can do to prepare. While looking the area over, he should compile a list of materials needed for building projects and mission projects. The calculation should be adjusted upward by approximately ten to fifteen percent (10-15%) for materials. It is extremely easy to underestimate the total cost of a project and be caught short. Large churches that take a lot of mission trips are experienced at calculating the costs necessary to complete the trip.

If flying to your mission remember you are a witness along the way at each airport and with each person. Traveling in this day and age can be stressful, but keep in mind those who wear shirts with your mission portrayed are walking billboards for the Lord. One angry or irritated word can undo the witness of your group.

CHAPTER 17

Starting Up Ministries

MOST OF OUR MINISTRIES BEGAN BY A NEED THAT AROSE and we would try to figure out how to meet it. Some of the needs that we addressed are listed here. Some of these things may be needs in your area also.

Go to the high school and speak with the athletic director. Don't go in with the attitude that says "I have something to show you". Go humbly and say, "Is there anything we can help with?" Here are some ideas that we have found churches can help with.

Offer to house athletic "away" teams in your church building -- Lighthouse does this. This will save the schools hotel costs. Talk to coaches before hand and offer to serve breakfast to teams. Determine a price per person that you could provide the breakfast for (be sure it is cheaper than they can get anywhere else). The teams appreciate good, healthy, balanced, filling breakfasts. When we served breakfast, we made it a full breakfast. A menu would include sausage, bacon, biscuits, eggs, and cereal. Additional items could be pancakes, French toast, and hash browns. Coaches are more than happy to have the meal provided and it gives the athletes a good start for the day at a minimal price to them. It might be necessary to have someone to cook, but usually you can persuade some to volunteer. The positive comments we received from schools far out-weighed any cost of breakfast or time that it took to provide it

One of the things I have found is people are more worried about buildings than they are about the ministry of souls. We don't preach to kids who come; we befriend them, leave tracts lying around and have appropriate scripture verses on the walls. They expect it will be there because they are staying in a church. We don't club anyone over the head with our Bibles, and knock them senseless so they will hear the Word of God. They have to feel the love of God in our actions, then you can look for opportunities to speak His words to them. Remember you are building a relationship so you can earn the right to talk to them. All the groups who have stayed in the church have left it clean and in order. Many people speak favorably of LCC around the state because of the hospitality the members have shown. We received many calls throughout the school year because word of mouth spread that the church is open.

Ask your local sports or scholastic directors if you can help with activities. Some of our men would be at the football game to help with the chains for the "downs". We enjoyed hosting a hospitality room during tournaments. A hospitality room has food and drinks available to the staff, coaches, and helpers. We put a little eight and a half by eleven and a half inch sign on the door stating, "Hospitality Room provided by Lighthouse Community Church". We kept it well stocked throughout the tournaments, from the time teams arrived until they quit at night. We always had someone sitting there, not necessarily to share the gospel, but to be available to answer questions. Sometimes members do have opportunities to answer questions about the church. When they are asked, "why do you do it?" then they can share God's love and their testimonies.

We have been able to start Bible Clubs in the schools. One teacher will let us use her room, and an adult will oversee it, but a student has to be in charge. We have Bible clubs in the High School, Junior High, and elementary schools. Nikiski Jr/Sr High School allows the community churches to use the school library one night a month, to gather and pray for the school, the teachers, and the students. Some schools may rent their facilities for use, so it may cost a little bit of money.

The schools, have on occasion, called the church and asked our members to operate their snack bar. Your school or PTA may need to recruit help. Some times they have trouble raising funds or recruiting people to run the snack bar. Do this and do it joyfully. We had them ask us to completely run the snack bar because no one else wanted to. The elementary school once called and asked for help with a fun day that was already scheduled but all their promised help had cancelled. Several of our church members came to the school and gladly helped out. One thing our staff knew was that if the school asked for anything, the answer was always "YES"! Then we figured out how to do it.

We bought clothes, coats, hats, and boots for those who didn't have them. We were asked to provide Christmas presents for children. We put out a plea to the churches in the "lower 48" states to help with gifts. Again, if your church is going to help a school, say "yes" to the need quickly and then figure out how to make it happen. When the schools see that you will make it happen then they will know that they can count on you. They will trust you.

By meeting needs like these and jumping through all kinds of hoops to do so, you will find that other ministries will open up to you. The community will see you are there to help, not wanting anything in return. No one will have to go out and "beat your church's drum" to tell what you are doing; everybody will see what your church is doing and what it stands for. During our sport camps, the principal many times would come out and just watch. She knew that these were "her kids" we were teaching. Our sports camps were publicized in the school and kids are invited to other church activities, through Bible Club in the high school. You can do a lot, but you start by asking how you can help, by being a servant. Find out what schools need the most help with, and then just help out. Don't expect thanks or even a positive response at first. Just try to be Jesus' hands and feet to your community.

By being visible in the school system and at community functions, children know the pastors and lay people. When they come to church, Sunday school, and youth group, they are comfortable and see familiar faces. They build a trust with these Christians and know when there is a crisis in their lives; these are they people they can turn to. There were many times during our ministry in Nikiski that children have turned to our church through the death of a parent, friend, or other life crisis.

The main thing is to ask God how to make things happen and GET ACTIVE!! God will show you how it can be done. You will find people who will support you in practical ways through all these efforts. Ministry is the key to reaching people. If you have a hundred ministries and you only reach one person per ministry, then you have reached one hundred more people. And praise God, you are going to win souls to the Lord. We began working with youth and children because this was the need presented to us.

One of our most successful ministries was our food ministry. We started by serving dinners at our house on Sunday night for all who attended the evening service. Following dinner thee members would gather to play games. It was a great time of bonding and fun. These dinners continued until we began having about forty-five weekly. We then began serving Wednesday evening dinner prior to mid-week service. We asked for donations of three dollars per person or ten dollars for a family. There was no "cashier" and donations were on honor basis. The donations just about covered the cost of the food. It was a great time of fellowship. Sometimes we had about three-quarters as many as on Sunday morning. Families could come to church without going home after work, because we did the cooking. They could enjoy a good meal, and they were already at church. This worked well for us.

Another ministry that had great appeal was drama. The children put on these productions. My wife directed the productions and Ashley McGee was the co-director. Several other volunteers helped make this ministry successful. Productions were performed twice a year. During Wednesday evening church time, practices were held. When the productions first began, the age group involved was first grade through sixth grade. As time went on and the children matured, it became "cool" for older kids to participate. Now the actors are first grade through twelfth grade. Often there are adults who fill parts. Practice for the Christmas program begins in August, when school starts and the program is presented right before Christmas. The kids then have about a month off and practice begins for the spring production. The spring program is presented right before school is out for the summer. The kids then have the summer off. Many times the only way family members came into the church building was through the drama program. It opens the door for ministry to parents and grandparents and others by performing a program that also presents the plan of salvation.

Another way to get into new ministries is to go to the local Chamber of Commerce. Pay the dues for your church to join and go to the luncheons. The special needs of the community are discussed at the meetings. By asking the Lord to reveal His will to you, you can find out what can be done to meet those needs. You may discover some needs that nobody else is doing anything about just by listening.

There are funds to be accessed to help you operate a food pantry. We were able to access funds through World Hunger. This is money that is routed through the Alaska Baptist Convention. We distributed food from the church, donated by our people and purchased from the food bank. Our food pantry ran that way for several years. A few years ago, the North Star United Methodist Church became actively involved with distributing food. Seeing we could better serve the community with one food distribution location in the area, we turned over our part of this ministry to the Methodists. Lighthouse continued to donate food to them and their church now handles this ministry in Nikiski.

God has blessed every effort, cementing our relationships with our schools, other churches, and the community at large.

Ministries that LCC has been involved in over the past thirteen years.

Preschool
Sunday School
Preschool Worship
Kids Night Out Program
Wednesday Evening Activities
Monday – Friday Preschool

Children
Sunday School
Children's Worship
Kids Night Out Program
Children's Activities
Monday-Friday School

Children/Youth
Wednesday Play Rehearsal

Youth
Sunday School
Boys Discipleship
Girls Discipleship
Thursday Night Youth Worship
Youth Evangelism Conferences
Winter Youth Celebration
World Changers (in & out of state)
Youth Retreat
Bible Studies at High School
Working On Elderly Housing

Youth/Adults
Worship
Kids Night Out Workers
Interpretive Dance
Local World Changer Support
Guitar Lessons
Praise Team

Adults
Sunday School
Wednesday Evening
Weekly Bible Studies
Women's Ministry
Spiritual Inventory Ministry
Prayer Ministry
Monthly All Night Prayer
Young Adult Sunday Evening

Community
Van Ministry
Food Pantry

Feeding Cannery Workers (past)
Senior Center Bible Study
Prison Bible Study
AA
Gideons
Elementary School Breakfast Program
Nikiski Community Services
Good Samaritans (help as needed)
Wednesday Night Meals
Hospitality Room at High School
Housing for High School Visiting Teams
Disaster Relief
Hosted North Peninsula Chamber of Commerce (2 years)
Senior's Club House
Friendship Rescue Mission (2005)

Agencies we help as needed
Red Cross
Crisis Pregnancy Center
Love, Inc.
Boys and Girls Club
United Way
Rock (local Crisis Group
Nikiski Senior Center
Alaska Community Development Corporation (rural develop)
USDA –United States Development of Agriculture
PAC-Public Advisory Committee for Alaska Housing Finance Co
Home School Group Meeting

Sports Camps
Soccer
Softball
Volleyball
Basketball

Archery

Lighthouse Community Church is to this day looking for and starting new ministries.

CHAPTER 18

Without A Vision The People Perish

IT SEEMS THERE ARE SOME WHO WOULD RATHER PAY SOMEONE to do ministry rather than perform the ministry himself or herself. God neither wants nor needs their money. He wants them! He wants them to be servants! It is hard to find people who have both money and the spirit to serve God. Every believer needs a willingness to serve God and to minister to the poor.

We need to minister to dysfunctional families, to families who are broken and torn apart. Churches need to wake up to the fact there are more blended families than not. We need to help these families because they experience more problems than most other families could imagine. There are financial problems; often children are split between two households, dealing with stepparents they might not get along with. The list goes on and on.

We must find ways to minister to the people who need us the most. We need ways to minister to those who don't have food. We must help people whose houses are falling apart and who don't have the means to fix it. We have to find ways to minister to a lost world, that they might come to know Jesus and His love for them. They need to know Him as their rescuer, their healer, their Lord.

CHAPTER 19

Do You Look Like A Horse?

I DON'T KNOW WHERE MY FATHER HEARD IT, BUT A favorite quote of his was: "If a person walks up to you and says you look like a horse, you can laugh it off. But if a second independent person walks up and says you look a horse, maybe you need to look in the mirror. If a third independent person walks up and says you look like a horse, you better go buy a saddle".

Some people think problems are because of everyone else. Many times problems are because of the person in the mirror. Generally, when three independent groups come and tell you the same thing, you have a problem. Maybe we are the ones who need to change. If a group of people get together and tell you there is a problem that is only one voice. But if three independent groups tell you the same thing, then you need to pay attention. You could be the problem.

I have met several preachers who have been in three or four different churches, and they talk about how bad those churches were. Perhaps these three, four, or five churches in which they were involved were that bad, but possibly those preachers need to look honestly at their own responsibility for their problems. There are churches that go through a pastor every one to two years. These churches may place the blame on "bad" pastors. Maybe the members need to look within and evaluate whether they need to change.

God may be trying to do something, but maybe they, the church

OR pastor, don't want to change. Churches who have been around for a long time could be undermining their effectiveness because they resist change. Change is taking place all around us and it doesn't need to be feared. It will take change to reach people especially younger people and those without a church background. We need to understand and respect that not everyone will respond to any one style of worship or ministry. We understand it in life and we must understand it in church.

Churches today have put God on a time schedule. If God can't do His work by noon, He is not going to work today. If He can't do His work in one service a week, why should we attend the rest of the services? I believe Sunday School is where you put all your best effort. If Sunday School grows, all the rest of your services will grow. But it is hard to get it growing. If you can't find the right mix of Bible study, music and activities, just try something different. Try something new and refreshing. You may find that one thing will work for children, another will work with youth, and yet another will work for adults. Do what ever it takes to win people to Christ.

Some church members have the attitude if people don't like what they find in the church service, they can go somewhere else. That is a problem; lost people are all going somewhere else and it isn't to church. Many of our churches no longer care for the lost, the needy, and the hurting enough to bring them to church and tell them about a Savior who loves them and gave His life for them.

Too many people want church to be what they want it to be, instead of letting God do what He wants to do. I can assure you what He wants to do is greater than yours and my grandest imaginations. Don't miss being a part of it.

Many people want to do things the way they used to. If you want to drive a car that is fifty years old that's ok, but you'll give up all the great new features. If you want to live in a house that is fifty years old think of the modern conveniences you won't have. Do you really want to get your food the way they did fifty years ago and eat what was available? I would imagine you probably enjoy going out to eat at restaurants that weren't around fifty years ago. If you do want to live in the past of fifty years ago, then you are unusual. If you have incorporated these new things in your life then why do you resist what is new in the church.

God wants to do a work in our churches. Are you one of those standing in the way of God's work? If you are then move aside and let leaders lead and preachers preach. Don't be a hindrance to God's work. Examine yourself and ask for God's guidance then surrender to His leading. Don't be a door stopper but a door opener. God uses many different ways to accomplish His work. Let Him work. You'll see God moving in a mighty way in your life and in the lives of others.

Sometimes we crush the Holy Spirit. We stop the Spirit's work because of the way we think things "ought to be done". Allow God to do a new work in a new way. The message can NEVER change but the methods can. It is easy to look at your congregation and see if it is more about you than about God. Where are the young people? Where are the children? Where are the families that are under the age of thirty? Look at yourself, add thirty years to your current age and then do the same with all of the people in the church. Think about who would be left after that thirty years. If more than two-thirds of the number are left, you may have a healthy church, if not within that time the church may die off with the members. Church should have enough young people and young families as a part that the work will go on. Ask God to reveal to you what needs to be done.

God's Word makes it clear. The only litmus test at Lighthouse was: Is it contrary to the Word of God? If it is contrary to the Word of God, then we are not going to do it! Every method, idea, program should be filtered through His Word. If someone has a burden for that ministry, then let's make it work! At Lighthouse, funds needed for a ministry had to be raised by the ones doing that ministry if we didn't have it in the budget. There are a lot of churches that have millions in their budget, but there are a lot more churches that are small and struggling to make ends meet. I believe that these small churches can have as big a heart, and do as much as many of the large ones. They must have a spiritual mind set for ministry. When they have that, God can only bless them.

CHAPTER 20

Building Buildings Without Money

HOW DO YOU BUILD BUILDINGS WITHOUT MONEY? HOW DO YOU survive in a church that has little income?

In December of 1996 the church in Nikiski didn't have much money, and the budget was small, under a hundred thousand dollars. They had twenty-two hundred dollars a month mortgage debt. That included bills, insurance, and salary. It didn't take long to exhaust what came in. In October, when the church members received the Permanent Fund checks, the church made up any deficits. These are checks paid out to each resident of Alaska, based on the earnings of the oil pipeline. Without this yearly boost of income, the church was nearly doomed.

The church building was a small building, having about three thousand square feet upstairs, and about the same downstairs. It was surrounded by woods with a very small parking lot holding maybe twenty cars. In the summer of 1997 several work teams came to Alaska. One team held Vacation Bible School; one team designed and painted the sign out front; and JR Hensley came and enlarged the parking lot by excavating the land. He and I decided to at least double the size. It wasn't too long before we filled it up. There was handicap access to the downstairs, but not to the upstairs because the building was built before handicap access was required. Next a work team came up and built the ramp to the auditorium.

By the second year we really needed to build a bigger building. We owed one hundred thousand dollars on the original building, and the assets of the church were four hundred and ninety-five thousand. We didn't have a whole lot to work with. We had the pews in the church, and a beautiful baby grand piano, donated by the pianist's mother. We had six wooden folding tables and forty-four metal folding chairs. The downstairs was just an open room. The fellowship hall was divided into four rooms. There were only three other rooms that could be used for Sunday school. I knew we needed more space, so I prayed and asked God to show me the answer.

Around that time, the loan officer of the Home Mission Board came to visit every church in Alaska that had loans with them. He told me on the phone before he arrived about the paperwork needed in order to get financing from loan department of the Home Mission Board to build the buildings we needed. I will never forget when he came into my office. I had all the paperwork he wanted to see spread out on my desk. He took about thirty seconds to look at it and said that HMB wouldn't give us the loan. Furthermore, he would not have given us our original loan based on these documents. I was a little aggravated. According to the records, the church had never been late on a payment, so I asked him why? He said, "You just don't have the income. You don't have the ability to repay the loan." I told him we were repaying the loan we had. He told me "You won't find anyone who will loan you the money." But, he said, "You are right. If you are going to grow, you will need a different building." I asked him how to do that, but he had no ideas. From that time I started praying and asking God to show me how to do it. I started applying to banks in Alaska to see if I could borrow the money. As soon as they saw the income, the discussion was over. We tried financial institutions all over the United States, and every time we got the same reaction. Nobody would touch this loan because we didn't have the assets or the income to secure it.

I began to ask God how to make this work for us. Then I got the bright idea of building just two rooms a year and eventually we would have all the rooms we needed. I went to the Southern Baptist Convention in Salt Lake City that year, and saw my old friend, Rick Ferguson, of the Riverside Baptist Church of Denver, Colorado. He was First Vice President of the Southern Baptist Convention that year. I said, "Rick, would you put me in contact with some pastors in your area?" He agreed, and he was always ready to lend a hand.

After one of the convention sessions, I met with Rick and a couple of pastors from his area. I had a drawing of the rooms we wanted to build and I asked them if they were interested in sending a work team to Alaska to help us build. They said yes. Then I told them there was a catch -- we didn't have any money. Could they bring five thousand dollars for material so we could build? I again showed them the drawing. To my surprise, they asked for a complete drawing they could use. They said I needed to be serious and build the space we needed and they would become the first three to sign up to help.

I began to pray and thank God. I was ashamed and had to ask God to forgive my lack of faith. I began to think about how to recruit other teams to help, but didn't know how to do this. I felt like a beggar and I had never begged in my life. God and I had to work through this idea of asking for help. He had an easier time of it than I did. God revealed to me that people cannot meet a need if they don't know about the need. He also showed me if it was a valid need, (and ours was a valid need,) then he would take care of it.

I made up a packet of information: all the financial records, the attendance records, the records of baptisms, and other pertinent information and put it on a spreadsheet. Then I wrote a short history of our church, where we were and how far we had come. I went to a garage sale and I bought a huge video recorder for fifty dollars. The battery was no good so I bought a hundred foot extension cord. I walked around the building, and made a video of why we needed to build. I walked all through the building, and showed all there was to see. I talked all the way through the video, talking about the church, and why we needed to build. I made up the packet to show we didn't have the resources to do the project ourselves, either in finances or manpower.

There had been times before I came to the church when they couldn't pay the bills. Sometimes they just fanned out the bills and asked the members if they would take one of the bills and pay it. People were actually doing this because they didn't receive enough offerings to pay the bills. We hardly had enough money to get by, but God always provided for us.

The Alaska Baptist State Convention had a partnership with the Georgia Baptist Convention.. By the end of the summer of 1999, we had seventeen teams who committed to come and bring five thousand dollars each. No one could have imagined this happening. Had I not swallowed my pride and followed the Lord's leading to ask for help, no one would have known to show up.

During that year and in the coming years we would be grateful to our Georgia partnership, especially Henry County, and also for our North Carolina partnership, particularly Mark Abernathy, when the Georgia partnership ended. These were vital to the success of our partnerships and the success of the alliance between LCC and so many work teams.

That year we built a two-story education building, which was forty-eight by forty-four feet. We also built fifteen-foot hallways upstairs and downstairs to connect to the existing building. All of these workers needed to be housed. We were able to scrounge up twenty-two twin size beds, and borrowed mattresses from everyone we could. I asked our members to bring in sheets, pillows, pillowcases, and blankets. We set up eleven beds with only about a foot of room to squeeze by and then set up eleven on the other side. We made a dormitory style room in the downstairs fellowship hall. The men and the women were divided by ceiling mounted room dividers. Every Saturday, the women of our church would come to wash the sheets and remake the beds for the next team to come in. Bathrooms and floors were cleaned and mopped and readied for the newcomers. We had enough room to set up three tables in the aisle between them. We served meals at those tables. It was extremely cramped, but no one seemed to mind.

That year we made so many mistakes. We fed three meals everyday, and we wore our members down physically and financially. We only had a handful of volunteers who could do the work and we learned those were some of the things we had to change.

When teams came and saw what our church was doing in the community, their hearts were touched, and they would donate even more money. Some went back to their churches and told the story of our church, and churches started sending us more funds. We broke ground for the new educational building on May 25, 1999. We were able to pour the foundation in a mono pour slab. When it was done there was no money left in the bank. We really didn't have enough to pay off what we did. I told the church at least we had an ice skating rink if nothing else happened. We were supposed to have more teams coming and bringing money, but we didn't know for sure.

One thing I learned was to get the money from the teams thirty days in advance so we could have the materials on the ground when they arrived. When I realized this was a problem I went to Home Depot, in Anchorage, about one hundred and seventy miles from us, and opened an account with them. They gave us a ten thousand dollar line of credit. During the course of the summer, I charged thirty thousand dollars on that card, three times. I didn't know how I was going to pay for it. I didn't know when we would get the money. I told Debbie I didn't know how, but if the money didn't come in from donations we would have to pay the bill. The monthly payment was around eight hundred dollars. I believed since I had charged it, we would have to take the responsibility, but God always saw that it was paid off—every time!!

One couple, the first to leave while I was there tested my faith a bit. I remember thinking, "How are we going to make it without their tithe and offerings." This is a fault of many pastors. I prayed and said "Lord, I understand that they need to move on, but we need those finances." They went to another church, and they were active there. They had done a great job in our church but said they just couldn't take the changes. The music was changing too much for them and they didn't like the fact that we were going to build a new building when we didn't have the money, especially since we didn't have enough money to meet the budget. They didn't feel that we could fill the space, and wondered why we were going to build bigger. Even though God moved them out, they remained our friends.

We learned so much through the process of building that building. By October thirteenth we used the building for the first time. The best part was that it was one hundred percent paid for! Every building or addition we have built has been built to commercial specifications, and we did it all for twenty-four to thirty dollars a square foot. I have actually bid out materials in five thousand dollar increments. On those increments there was always a two thousand dollar difference between the high and low bids. I would make a list of the needed materials and fax it out to five or six places, and the lowest bids usually came from the Anchorage area. I would take the seats out of the fifteen-passenger van, attach a trailer behind and spend all day in Anchorage picking up materials. Then I would drive back, loaded way past what that van should have pulled. I don't know how many trips I made that year to get materials to build the first addition.

God blessed us and we made it. God saw us through it. We thought it was going to kill us, but it didn't. One thing I believe is if you are going to build a building you need to do it as quickly as possible. People from a small church can't afford to look at an unfinished building they can't use the discouragement wears on them. Everything we have built, has been started in May and been finished by October.

God has blessed us so much with the teams who came to help us build Lighthouse Community Church. I have learned so much through the process, it has been amazing. The point I want to make is this: Until we stepped out in faith, we didn't see God's hand at work. When we stepped out in faith we saw God working in ways we never could have imagined.

The most efficient way to communicate the tasks that were completed and accomplishments of LCC are to form a time line. Visuals can many times illustrate what words cannot.

These are the highlights of Lighthouse Community Church over the past thirteen years.

The church called Denver & Debbie Copeland on December 20, 1996. Under his leadership and by God's grace and provision, the following has been accomplished:

-1997 A new sound system was installed in the church. A larger sign and reader board was installed, a handicap ramp built, and the parking lot expanded to twice the original size.

-1998 Trees to the south of the building were cleared, a circular driveway added, and the parking lot again doubled in size.

-1999 Approximately 4,500 sq ft education building was built. New outside lighting was installed. Community Appreciation Day held which fed over 500 people.

-2000 The original church building was totally remodeled, both upstairs and downstairs. A new entryway was built with a covered drive. The front of the sanctuary was extended and a stage built.

-2001 A 420 sq ft storage shed was built. A 125 sq ft lower floor entryway was added between the buildings.

-2002 The parsonage built (2,800 sq ft with 1,200 sq ft garage), A 15 x 12' bedroom was added to the youth pastor's apartment.

-2003 A shower trailer was built, consisting of 8 stalls and its own boiler system; we also built a 16 sq ft storage building. The preschool opened in August, with Ginnie Handley, Preschool Administrator. We purchased 10 acres adjacent to church property.

-2004 We added an additional 1,500 sq ft education space to building that was built in 1999. We built a 3,400 sq ft administration/youth building with 1,000 sq ft Youth Pastor's apartment. An elementary school was added to existing Preschool. We added a mobile laundry facility.

-2005 The rear of the sanctuary was extended 12' and a handicap restroom, cry room, and sound room added at the entry. We created a recreation area consisting of softball/baseball field, volleyball court, basketball court, soccer/football field, picnic area, and two horse shoe pits (½ mile walking track will be added in 2006) (It may take up to 2 years to finish the recreation area and hope that within the next five years a full-size gymnasium for community use will be built.

-2006 Work teams built a house for Pastor Denver's family and Pastor Randy moved into the parsonage in mid August 2006. During the summer we conducted 5 sports camps, and had 110 children in VBS.

-2007 Purchased 6 acres with a 30'X50' building, drilled a well, put in the septic system, built in bathrooms with 2 showers. Built small efficiency cottage to house volunteers. Conducted 7 sports camps and VBS.

-2008 Built 5 24'X24' cabins on 6 acres and built a new front entry to the church approximately 20'X24'. Conducted 7 sports camps, VBS, and began archery.

Since the beginning of the church, Backyard Bible Clubs/VBS have been conducted annually. 2008 was the 7th year of World Changers in the Nikiski area. 2008 completed the 9th year that our church has been involved in the breakfast program and the second year for Good News Clubs at the elementary schools in Nikiski.

Over 75 work teams have helped in all that God has accomplished.

CHAPTER 21

Steppin' Out

I believe Lighthouse Community Church, by stepping out in faith, has seen modern day miracles, one after the other. A lot of people wouldn't consider them miracles, but I believe they are just that. I believe miracles are things that we can't get done under our own power, but it is God's work alone. He empowers us and shows us how to do things that we could never accomplish on our own. Every building built, every acre of land purchased, every program started, every sports camp held, and almost every other ministry of the church were all accomplished when we didn't have the resources to do it. But God always provided. We only had to be available and willing to get out and work at His leading.

I believe these are all modern day miracles, and people today are not use to seeing miracles. You may say it is not like a miracle something just appearing, but it is if you don't have the ability to make it appear. Are we walking by sight or are we walking by faith? I would much rather walk by faith than by sight. I do not ever want to be limited by my feeble sight.

You may say there are so many churches, why should anyone care about Nikiski? My answer is put your own church's name in that statement? I can tell you who cares: God cares about a little church in Nikiski. I can tell you who will provide the needs: God will.

Some when they read this book will say it might work there, but it will never work here. I can guarantee if you believe it won't work, it won't. When you get the word "never" out of your vocabulary, you will see what God can do. You will see God do things you never dreamed. You will see God's hand moving everywhere.

You will not get it done saying, "God can never do that here". Pastor, you will never get it done saying, "God will never allow that to happen". Church member, you will never see it happen if you say, "God will never work like that here". Leaders, if you say, "It can't be done here", it won't. You must believe that God is, and He rewards those who seek him.

When we can pray in one accord, and say, "God, we need something different", we will see the hand of God moving and working in our lives and our churches. We can't keep on doing the same old thing and expect to get different results. We need to want what God wants. Don't make a laundry list of what you want, or a list of what you hope for. Ask God to show you what He wants to do in your life. Let God show you what needs to happen. If you are an older person, allow younger people to come up with some ideas. Maybe you can't see the vision but please don't stand against it. They need your wisdom, and they are your wisdom. They need your experience. Allow God to work. Remember, if God is in it, it will work, if He is not in it, it won't work no matter how hard we try. Allow God to control things and do not try to put a stop to it.

CHAPTER 22

Lord, We Will Stay Forever

DURING THE WINTER OF **2005** AND INTO THE SPRING OF 2006 we had prayed and felt God may possibly allow us to stay in Nikiski until death or retirement, whichever came first.

It was during that winter I began to feel that we needed to put down some "roots" and do some planning for our future. As many pastors have, I realized continuing to live in a parsonage was leaving us without a home of our own or investment for retirement years. I am a firm believer that God gives us the desire to care for our families and ourselves in those later years.

Debbie and I purchased a two-acre plot of land and planned to build our retirement home on it. That winter I firmed up our construction loans and began the process of building. During those months of planning and preparation to build, many of the churches whose teams had helped us in prior years began calling and asking what projects we had going for the summer of 2006. I would tell them none, because we were building our personal home. Many of them indicated they would be happy to come and assist us in the construction. We were thrilled and humbled again by God's provision.

By August 15, 2006, we moved into our dream home. We constructed it to be everything we wanted in a home for then and the coming years. As we moved into this home, Randy and Destiny Lewis moved into the parsonage. Our family had shrunk to just the two of us and theirs consisted of six children and they needed the space. The Lord had provided for both families.

A side note here…Prior to the Lewis' attending LCC, Randy had said that he would not attend a church where the pastor needed that large a house. God has a great sense of humor! Randy now lives in that very house with his family and is thankful for all of the space it affords them.

Little did we know at the time that God would use even our beautiful house to bring about His purpose in our lives.

CHAPTER 23

The Rest of the Story

FOLLOWING HURRICANE KATRINA, BUBBA BROUSSARD AND I, WENT TO ASSIST with the Disaster Relief effort. After I returned to Alaska, Bubba stayed for several months and worked in Disaster Relief kitchens, leading teams who were feeding survivors of the storm.. It was Bubba who met Pastor Gary Yaufso from Aina Haina Baptist Church, Oahu, Hawaii.

As he got to know them and talked with them, they shared that work groups would frequently come to help with the ministry at Aina Haina Baptist Church and some would also work at Pu'u Kahea Baptist Conference Center. Bubba called me and asked what I thought about taking a work team to Hawaii. How could I turn this down? We would gain great insight from being members of a work team instead of the hosts for a change. It would be a good way to "pass on" the blessings we had received from the teams who had helped us. And what better way to get a group of people to go on a mission trip from Alaska than to take them to Hawaii! I told him to sign us up.

In November of 2007, eight members of Lighthouse Community Church, along with Bubba's nephew, Beau Broussard and my sister Nadine Priest, from Kentucky went to Pu'u Kahea Baptist Conference Center. One thing we quickly learned is that if you are going to Hawaii on a mission trip, no one buys it. They won't even pray for you! They are envious and think you are going for a vacation.

It was not a vacation. Our group painted and worked on the roof and eaves of the third floor of the Plantation Hale (House). This historic building is ninety-nine years old and was in need of upkeep.

As I was working on the roof, the Lord impressed on my heart that this is where we would be ministering next. I was fine with that, I just felt as though it would be in the distant future, after retirement but God would not let me go. So, I began to ask questions of Furman Toney, the director at that time. I was sure if I would just ask just the right questions, God would free me from thinking about it.

My main concern was this was probably a volunteer position and only retired couples with an independent income would be financially able to fill the position. Furman told me the director position was in fact a paid position and although the salary was not one to get rich on, a couple could survive. The next thing he said to me shook me to my core. He confided that he would be retiring soon and leaving Pu'u Kahea no later than February 2009. It was though God whispered in my ear "either put up or shut up!" Every concern I had was invalid and God had opened another unexpected door.

That Sunday as we sat in the sanctuary at Waianae Baptist Church, I turned to Deb and said, "I really feel like we will be here someday." She said, "I know, God has been working on me too!"

We went back home to Nikiski and I asked the church to pray for us and for God's will because I felt we would be leaving the church in November 2008. Everyone will tell you not to give a church a year's notice, but we did.

In February, Deb and I returned to Hawaii to pray and investigate all the details of moving and to meet with the Executive Director of the Hawaii Baptist Convention. It was a favorable meeting and we returned home and began the process of getting our house ready to sell and preparing to move.

We put our house on the market in May 2008. As we prepared it for sale, many told us that a house of that value would take quite a while to sell as the market was beginning to crash. The purchasers chose the closing date, August 15, 2008, exactly two years to the day from when we moved in. God even took care of our compliance with the two-year IRS rule regarding capital gains on the sale of our house! Due to the proceeds of the sale, we were able to pay off debt and be financially able to live on the salary provided at Pu'u Kahea. The Lord has met every need we have had in the past and for the present and we know He will continue to do so in the future.

We returned to Hawaii in September, 2008 for training and for confirmation of hiring by the Hawaii Pacific Baptist Executive Board. They voted to have us become directors effective December 1, 2008.

On November 1, we left Nikiski and the best church and pastorate I have ever been blessed to work in. At the time of our departure we had grown to approximately 150 to 165. Our budget had grown from under $80,000 to $165,000 and the church had been self-supporting for three to four years.

As we look forward to what the Lord is going to accomplish in Waianae, Hawaii our hearts are filled with expectation and excitement. We hit the ground running December 1st and have already seen many things accomplished, even in the short time since we arrived. Lighthouse Community Church has remained close and brought a team of men to come and work on the remodel of the home that we now live in. The volunteers who come monthly to give of their time and energy to help in this ministry have blessed us.

The Executive Board has approved plans to build four new buildings at Pu'u Kahea Baptist Conference Center. We are also beginning a capital campaign to raise a half a million dollars ($500,000.) to accomplish this goal. As was the case at LCC, I have no idea how God intends to bring this to pass, but I know that He will and we will be here to gladly be His hands and His feet.

Through the ministry of the conference center, many people have come to the Lord, have grown in Him and have gone out to reach others for Him. Although this is a very different type of ministry for me, I've discovered Pu'u Kahea is a place of renewal and commitment, vital to the spiritual growth of those who come here, whether to work or for retreat.

Since December, several work teams have come to work on the buildings and to minister to the neighborhood. They tell us they are greatly blessed by being here even when the work is hard. They and others have reported over sixty conversions through conferences, sports camps or backyard Bible clubs just since the first of the year.

Deb and I aren't at all surprised; we know who He is and we've seen Him work miracles. We just wait on Him, humbly and with great anticipation, to see all He will accomplish as people meet with Him in this place.

CHAPTER 24

Cookin' For A Group

I HAVE HAD PEOPLE ASK ME ABOUT RECIPES FOR COOKING for a large crowd. I would be glad to send them to you if you want to begin that ministry. I usually use full size disposable steam table pans. We get them at Sam's Club or Cost-Co. They come about fifteen to a pack and cost about eighty cents a piece. The reason I use them is I don't wash dishes. I make a meal just using several large serving spoons and I rinse them off and use them again. I do use hot water to sterilize them. I mix everything in the pans and I cook them in the oven. If you use the top of the stove you can have a mess to clean up. You can easily fix food for up to one hundred in one oven. Remember to practice good food handling principles.

NOTE: All "pans" in the following recipes refer to steam table pans, mentioned above.

Beef with Gravy and Vegetables
Buy a bottom grade of meat, sirloin or bottom roast, anything *except a seven-bone roast*. Most meat departments will slice it free, so have them slice it about one half inch thick, and then cut those in half. Figure about eight ounces of meat per person.

*To prepare the meat, season it with Lawry's and garlic salt.

* Prepare Gravy Mix. (I use a large containers of brown gravy mix: I put it in a drinking glass about half full and then

fill it up with water and mix. It looks like a paste and I spread it over the meat. You can make as many layers of meat and gravy paste as you need. I spread the paste on very thin. This makes the gravy as it cooks the meat.)

*Peel the potatoes and cut them into quarters and put them in a pan with some baby carrots, cover it with foil.

*Cook it in the oven for about three hours at 300 degrees.

This can be put in the oven before church, because it won't matter if it cooks a little longer or not. It will be tender enough to cut with a fork.

*This can also be done with chicken. Buy boneless chicken breast and cut them in half. Make a paste out of poultry gravy, add potatoes and carrots and cover it.
Bake at 300 for 3 hours.

We usually put it out in the pans and let people serve themselves. It really is easy to do.

Chicken Parmesan

*Take boneless chicken breast portions and season with Lawry's put them in a pan
*Cover them with spaghetti sauce
*Cover with foil
*Bake in the oven for three hours at approximately 300 degrees.

*When it is done take it out, open it and cover it with mozzarella cheese.
*Put it back in the oven until the cheese melts.

Green Chili Chicken Enchiladas

Another easy recipe to fix is Green Chili Chicken Enchiladas. You need flour tortillas, as many as you will be feeding times 2.

*Chop up the chicken in very small pieces, put a little olive oil in a pan, chop an onion or two, (figure approximately a quarter pound of chicken per person).

*Cook the chicken, add the seasoned cooked chicken to the pan, with onions, add some diced green chilies and cream cheese.

*Use green enchilada sauce and cover the bottom of the baking pan.

*Roll a large spoon full of chicken mix in the tortillas and put it in the pan.

*Pour the rest of the green sauce over the top of it.

*Cover with shredded cheddar cheese, and put it in the oven to melt the cheese.

Serve with refried beans and rice.

White Chili

If you make up a double portion of the chicken sauce them you can take what is left over

*Add chicken broth and sour cream.
*Add Monterrey Jack cheese.
*When that is thick enough add Great White Northern beans. Canned beans are ready to add.

This makes a very good soup.

ENCHILADAS

Another recipe is to get some red enchilada sauce, olive oil, flour or corn tortillas, hamburger meat and onions.

*Fry the hamburger and onions in oil.
*Place red sauce in the bottom of the pan
*Roll tortillas with the hamburger
*Cover with red sauce
*Cover with cheese
*Put in the oven, bake at 300 for 3 hours

I guess you can tell I never measure anything I just make what I think we need. If you would like more recipes, just send me an e-mail and I would be happy to give you more. denver@pkcc.org.

If you are interested in helping Lighthouse Community Church you can reach them at this address:

PO Box 7496
Nikiski, Alaska   99635

Phone # 907-776-8234

Current Website: www.lccak.com (this may be changing soon)

If you are interested in helping Pu'u Kahea Baptist Conference Center or contribute to the Building Fund, the address is as follow:

PO Box 467
Waianae, Hawaii 96792

Phone # 808-696-3467

Current Website: www.pkcc.org

Lighthouse Community Church
2007 Budget
January through December 2007

Accounts	Annual	Annual
01. Coop. Program 10%		$16,000.00
02. Association (314)		$600.00
03. Local Ministries (306)		$600.00
04. Missions Offering (303)		$600.00
05. FNBA (church loans)		$22,068.00
06. Literature		$500.00
14. Admin/office		$500.00
15. Utilities		$20,638.00
16. Church Insurance (312)		$7,000.00
18. Kitchen/Janitorial Supplies		$500.00
20. Pastor's Housing Allowance		$37,388.00
21. Pastor's Car Reimb.		$4,992.00
23. Pastor's Annuity (retirement)		$7,800.00
26. Youth Pastor Salary		$13,600.00
27. Youth Pastor's Annuity		$1,260.00
28. Youth Pastor's Medical Reimb.		$2,400.00
Housing/utilities/auto		furnished
29. Children's Pastor		$13,000.00
30. Children's Pastor Annuity		$1,260.00
Autos and housing		furnished
Totals:		$150,966.00

THANK YOU

WE THANK THE LORD DAILY FOR OUR CHILDREN AND GRANDCHILDREN.
Norman was grown when we came to Nikiski. He is currently living in Missouri.

Kelli moved to the Nikiski area for a time before returning to Missouri. On February 25, 2009, Kelli went home to be with the Lord. Although we do not understand, we know that God has His plan. Kelli has 2 children, Logan and Kassi. They live with their Dad in Missouri.

Michelle graduated from Nikiski High School. She is married to Jacob Hall and they have 3 children, Audrey, Phoenix, Aurora and a baby on the way. They are living outside of Atlanta, Georgia.

Jeanette graduated from Nikiski High School. She is married to Jesse Tapley and they have 2 sons, Ezekiel and Titus. They are living in Kenai, Alaska.

Kimberly graduated from Nikiski High School. She is married to Jeff Curren and they have 1 daughter, Peighton and a baby on the way. They live in Nikiski.

I want to thank those who pray for us. For those who have gone on and those who are still active in the church.

Many thanks to all who have read this account and have encouraged, persistently encouraged, edited, suggested, and encouraged some more to see this through to completion. Each of you knows who you are—thanks!

I am very thankful for the group of pastors that meet with our staff in Nikiski:

Wayne Coggins: North Kenai Chapel
Harold Lewis: First Baptist, Port Nikiski
Laura Skiba: North Star United Methodist Church
Paul Hartley: Church of the Nazarene
Randy Harris: Inlet Faith Assembly of God
Henry Haney: New Hope Christian Fellowship

We have met weekly and pray for God to transform the community and for God to send revival in our churches.

Thank you to the Baptist Conventions of North Carolina and Georgia. They have helped Lighthouse Community Church through a partnership. Special thanks to Mud Creek Baptist Church, NC who came to Nikiski countless times helping not only with building projects, but also with VBS and Sports camps. They have also been available with just a call to help with many financial needs in our community. Also, many thanks to First Baptist, Merryville, TN and Brushy Creek Baptist church, SC as they both came many times and assisted with building and financial needs. The Lord has provided through their people many miraculous blessings.

Also the countless churches and individuals, too many to list here, that have come and done as the Lord instructed. To you, we give our thanks and sincere appreciation

SERVICE

I have served in many positions in the Alaska Baptist Convention:
First Vice President
XO Member of the Missions Committee
XO Member of the Administrations Committee
Constitution and By Laws Committee as Chairman
Time, Place, and Preacher Committee as Chairman
Credentials Committee as Chairman
Executive Director Search Committee as Chairman
The Alaska Baptist Foundation as President
Nikiski Community Services as chairman
The Board of the Local Red Cross
The Board of Friendship Rescue Mission in Kenai, Alaska
Public Advisory Committee Alaska Housing Finance Corporation

Many of these positions I held while in the pastorate at Lighthouse Community Church. These experiences and relationships have enriched me personally and opened doors of service for LCC. For that I am so grateful.